MW00580670

WILDFIRE

BRITISH COLUMBIA BURNS

WILDFIRE

written by **CHARLES ANDERSON** & **LORI CULBERT**

edited by **SHELLEY FRALIC**

GREYSTONE BOOKS
Douglas & McIntyre Publishing Group
Vancouver/Toronto

CanWest Global
Communications Corp.

Copyright © 2003 by the *Vancouver Sun* and *Province*
newspapers, representing the Pacific Newspaper Group and
CanWest Global Communications

03 04 05 06 07 5 4 3 2 1

All rights reserved. No part of this book may be reproduced, stored in
a retrieval system or transmitted, in any form or by any means, without the prior
written consent of the publisher or a licence from the Canadian
Copyright Licensing Agency (Access Copyright). For a copyright licence, visit
www.accesscopyright.ca or call toll free to 1-800-893-5777.

Co-published by Greystone Books, the *Vancouver Sun* and the *Province*

Greystone Books
A division of Douglas & McIntyre Ltd.
2323 Quebec Street, Suite 201
Vancouver, British Columbia
Canada v5T 4S7
www.greystonebooks.com

National Library of Canada Cataloguing in Publication Data
Anderson, Charles, 1958–
Wildfire: B.C. burns / Shelley Fralic, editor; Charles Anderson
and Lori Culbert, writers; Nick Procaylo and Ian Smith, photo editors;
Kate Bird, project researcher.
Co-published by the *Vancouver Sun* and *Province*.

ISBN 1-55365-057-3

1. Forest fires—British Columbia. 2. Fires—British Columbia.
3. Fire fighters—British Columbia. I. Fralic, Shelley, 1953– II. Culbert, Lori, 1967–
III. Procaylo, Nick IV. Smith, Ian, 1950– V. Bird, Kate VI. Title.
SD421.34.C3A54 2003   363.37′9   C2003-906674-6

Editing by Shelley Fralic
Production editing by Anne Rose
Jacket and text design by Peter Cocking
Front jacket photograph by Gordon Bazzana
Back jacket photograph by Brian Sprout
Frontispiece photo: Kyle Sanguin battles the Okanagan
Mountain Park fire; photo by Cory Bilecki/firefighter
Printed and bound in Canada by Friesens
Printed on acid-free paper

We gratefully acknowledge the financial support of the Canada Council
for the Arts, the British Columbia Arts Council, and the Government
of Canada through the Book Publishing Industry Development Program (BPIDP)
for our publishing activities.

CONTENTS

FOREWORD / *2*

PROLOGUE / *5*

KAMLOOPS & AREA / *19*

McLure, Barriere,
Louis Creek, McGillivray

KELOWNA & AREA / *55*

Naramata, Okanagan Falls,
Osoyoos, Penticton

CRANBROOK & AREA / *103*

Lamb Creek, Plumbob Mountain,
Nelson, Fernie

EPILOGUE / *113*

ACKNOWLEDGEMENTS / *138*

FOREWORD

T HE IMAGES will stay with us forever. The colours: orange, red, black and grey—intense and foreboding. The power: fierce, destructive and unstoppable. The flames: searing and all-consuming, relentless infernos that incinerated houses, orchards, cars, businesses, parks and forests in minutes. Day after day, these images in our newspapers and on our televisions were so overpowering that they were almost impossible to fathom.

For from late in the spring into the fall of 2003, British Columbians stood in awe as Mother Nature, in a wild, supreme show of force, played no favourites, striking both communities and vast tracts of the province's forests, leaving nothing in her wake but smoke and ash and despair. More than 2,500 fires burned, devastating hundreds of thousands of hectares. The losses have been inestimable, both personal and historical, from the smallest toy owned by a child to the historic Kettle Valley Railway trestles cherished by generations. Three brave men, all pilots, lost their lives fighting the fires.

It was the summer in which dreams were lost and heroes made, the summer we learned that material things matter not nearly as much as family, friends and community. And we were reminded of a harsh lesson: that technology and even the most Herculean of human efforts are seldom a match for nature's alchemy of lightning, wind, drought and tinder-dry trees. It was the summer we discovered the stuff of which British Columbians are made.

The wildfires of 2003 tested our patience, our nerves and our faith. We faced anguish, terror, loss, regret and anger. And we stood in wonder in the face of true heroism, demonstrated by the community leaders who choreographed the battle against the firestorms, the thousands of

Coin box:
$1.50
Outside
Lower
Mainland: $1.87 minimum
$1.40 incl. tax

SUNDAY Province Sports Final c
Vancouver, B.C. • August 31, 2003 • www.theprovince.com
Mainly sunny
High 23
Low 13
Details, E40

THE DAY HELL CAME TO KELOWNA

'Guys, we're going to die'

That was the cellphone call that came in from a group of firefighters as the Kelowna firestorm roared down Okaview Road. Stunned residents and firefighters tell the story of their day of horror on the street they're calling 'ground zero' after 41 houses were razed   **Pages A10-12**

Nick Procaylo — The Province
Firefighters in the Okaview Road area of south Kelowna suddenly found themselves surrounded by 100-metre-tall flames on Aug. 22. Somehow, they got out.

men and women—professional and volunteer—who risked their lives on the front lines and the thousands of selfless volunteers and well-wishers from all over the province and the rest of Canada who donated money, goods and their precious time.

At this writing, late in the fall of 2003, just weeks after the last major fire was declared under control and while floodwaters are rising in communities on B.C.'s southwestern coast, there are still more than 200 forest fires burning. But history has shown that this province and its people are resilient, and already the rebuilding has begun. From Bonaparte Lake to McGillivray, from Louis Creek to Strawberry Hill, from Cranbrook to Okanagan Mountain Park, from Vaseux Lake to Hell's Gate, we have picked up the pieces, given Mother Nature her due and started over.

If the best newspapers, when held up to scrutiny, mirror their communities not only with accuracy and acuteness but with compassion, then our role must surely include opportunity for reflection on the significant events that change our lives. And so, we at the *Vancouver Sun* and *Province* newspapers, representing the Pacific Newspaper Group and CanWest Global Communications, present this book in commemoration of the long, hot summer of 2003—a summer that British Columbians won't soon forget.

DENNIS SKULSKY
President & Publisher, Pacific Newspaper Group
General Manager, B.C. Mainland Region
CanWest Canadian Media

"The smoke just goes on and on.

It's on such a scale that I wish I could describe it.

The forces of nature are incredible, and . . .

beyond my ability to describe."

GORDON CAMPBELL, premier of B.C.,

after an August 22 aerial tour of the devastation

PROLOGUE

THE WARNING SIGNS were all there.

As 2003's warm spring rolled into glorious summer, the record books showed that British Columbia hadn't seen anything like it in 74 years. A mild winter had denuded the mountains of much of the snowcap that traditionally soaks the ground and fills the streams come thaw. And as June slipped into July, week after week of sunshine and warmth saturated the forests, browning the undergrowth and baking the needles that lay in thick blankets beneath the ponderosa pine and Douglas fir. The sunshine wasn't unusual—especially for the British Columbia Thompson-Okanagan. But the combination of record temperatures with an unusually dry winter was.

In the province's Interior, the three months of June, July and August saw a total of only 23.6 millimetres of rainfall. Kelowna went 44 days without rain while, over the same period, Kamloops received just 3.3 millimetres—one-seventeenth its usual quota. As the dry months passed, forest officials scanned the statistics and grew increasingly worried. It was shaping up to be the province's driest summer since 1929, and the ground was tinder dry—a landscape of fuel. British Columbia's last severe fire season had been in 1998, and, after four benign years, it looked like the region's string of good luck was about to change. Still, no one anticipated the devastation to come.

FACING PAGE: Firefighter in action in the Lakeshore Drive area of Kelowna on Friday afternoon, August 22, 2003. *Nick Procaylo/the Province*

By the time the statisticians finished assessing the damage, the 2003 fire season was down in the books as one of British Columbia's most costly natural disasters. More than 2,500 infernos had burned a fiery swath across the southern part of the province, from Vancouver Island to Cranbrook and from Osoyoos to north of Fort Nelson. In total, 266,135 hectares went up in smoke despite the efforts of more than 10,000 professional firefighters and emergency personnel, brought in from around the province and across the country. The cost to the province for fighting the fires has been estimated at about $550 million; the cost of property loss, insurance claims and economic hardship remains impossible to calculate. The magnitude of the disaster is equally difficult to grasp. The largest fire of the year, at Midwinter Lake, was still active in late October 2003. At 32,000 hectares, the blaze was bigger than the major fires at Chilko Lake, McLure-Barriere and even Okanagan Mountain Park. But its isolation was such that, by the end of the fire season, hardly anyone had heard of it.

For in B.C. in 2003, almost every provincial wildfire record was broken. Homes and businesses lay burned. Vast tracts of forest larger than some countries were charred and thousands of B.C. households scarred. In many cases, lives were completely uprooted—families lost their homes and belongings and were forced to live in hotels or with relatives. Jobs were lost when businesses burned, and tourists stayed away. B.C. premier Gordon Campbell, who toured by helicopter both the McLure fire and Okanagan Mountain Park blaze, reported, "I continue to be struck by the size, the magnitude, the scale," after touring the Kelowna region. "The smoke just goes on and on and on. It goes north, it goes east. It's on such a scale that I wish I could describe it." The rest of B.C. watched the televised scenes from the Thompson-Okanagan in horrified fascination, as the perils of the parched Interior were brought home—even to the edge of the coastal rainforest—by a series of back-country travel advisories that matured into outright bans. For the first time in memory, would-be hikers were told to stay off the province's trail systems. There were simply no firefighters available to tackle any more fires caused by careless humans.

But if the wildfires of 2003 showed the worst of Mother Nature, they brought out the best in human nature. At the peak of the fire season, nearly 6,000

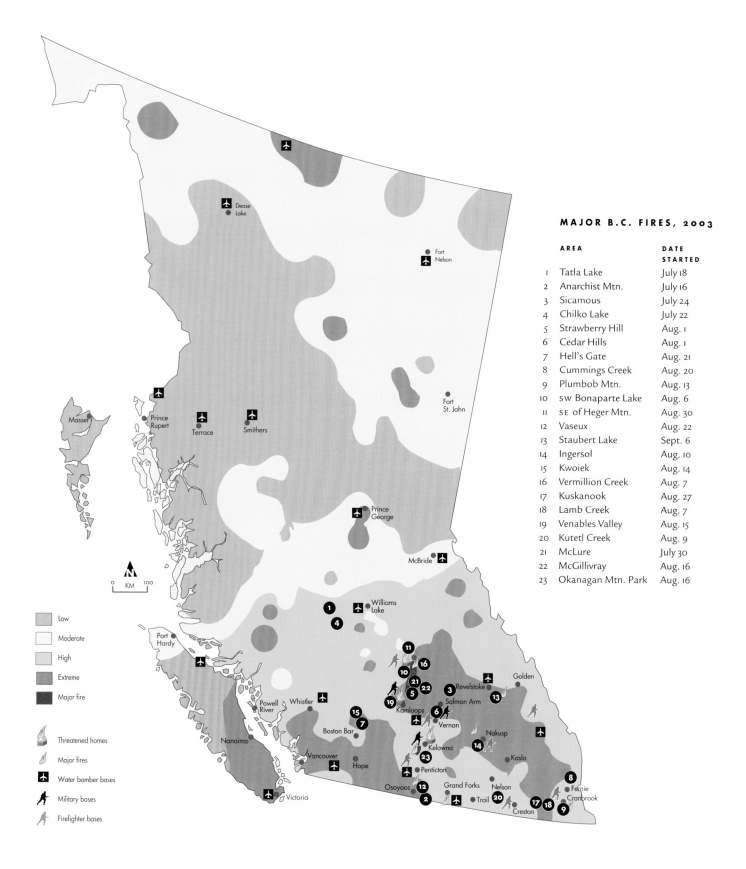

MAJOR B.C. FIRES, 2003

	AREA	DATE STARTED
1	Tatla Lake	July 18
2	Anarchist Mtn.	July 16
3	Sicamous	July 24
4	Chilko Lake	July 22
5	Strawberry Hill	Aug. 1
6	Cedar Hills	Aug. 1
7	Hell's Gate	Aug. 21
8	Cummings Creek	Aug. 20
9	Plumbob Mtn.	Aug. 13
10	SW Bonaparte Lake	Aug. 6
11	SE of Heger Mtn.	Aug. 30
12	Vaseux	Aug. 22
13	Staubert Lake	Sept. 6
14	Ingersol	Aug. 10
15	Kwoiek	Aug. 14
16	Vermillion Creek	Aug. 7
17	Kuskanook	Aug. 27
18	Lamb Creek	Aug. 7
19	Venables Valley	Aug. 15
20	Kutetl Creek	Aug. 9
21	McLure	July 30
22	McGillivray	Aug. 16
23	Okanagan Mtn. Park	Aug. 16

Low
Moderate
High
Extreme
Major fire

Threatened homes
Major fires
Water bomber bases
Military bases
Firefighter bases

ABOVE: Provincial fire control officer John Flanagan in the Provincial Fire Centre in Victoria on August 26, 2003. *Bruce Stotesbury/the Victoria Times-Colonist*

FACING PAGE: Jo Palmer, right, and forest technician Erik Nelson guard the entrance to Foley Lake, a popular camping spot in the Chilliwack River Valley closed due to the extreme fire danger. *Mark van Manen/the Vancouver Sun*

firefighters from across B.C. and Canada fought more than 2,500 fires, while Canada's military poured its forces into the regions most affected; some 2,600 reserves and regulars made Operation Peregrine the second-largest deployment after Afghanistan. With forestry service and emergency staff bolstering these numbers, in total more than 10,000 emergency personnel were brought into the Interior and southeastern B.C. from all over the province and the rest of Canada. Tens of thousands more throughout the province volunteered, serving without official designation while offering their homes, food, clothes, muscles and cold hard cash. The capacity for British Columbians to help each other has seldom been tested as it was in the summer of 2003. And they came through.

SUCH WAS THE SCALE and number of its wildfires that the B.C. forest fire season of 2003 is also a summer of statistics. By how many hectares did each fire grow? How many firefighters were deployed? How much heavy equipment was used? How many aircraft were committed? As the extent of the destruction became clear, the public was informed daily of these stats and more: the number of volunteers, the value and volume of donations, the number of evacuees, the number of homes destroyed and, most poignant, the number of men who gave their lives: three pilots flying aerial bombers and helicopters in an exhausting shuttle of skim, bomb, turn and skim.

On July 16, well before the midsummer mayhem, pilots Ian Mackay, 41, of Rossland, and co-pilot Eric Ebert, 36, of Toronto, died while firefighting some 10 kilometres southeast of the Cranbrook airport. Their four-engine Lockheed Electra aerial bomber had been tackling a small blaze when it crashed into a mountainside. Mackay left a wife and four children; Ebert was single. On August 17, helicopter pilot Ben von Hardenberg, 33, from Mission, crashed while fighting a fire near Bonaparte Lake just east of 100 Mile House. He died less than two weeks before he was to marry his girlfriend, Shawna, and move to Australia.

Looking back, the miracle of 2003 is perhaps that, with so many firefighters and volunteers deployed so closely to the fickle fire lines, more lives weren't lost. Yet the human and financial toll on the people of the Interior has been staggering. Provincial officials estimate the cost of fighting the fires at about $550 million—almost 10 times the figure anticipated in the government's 2003 firefighting budget. The final cost of homes destroyed and lives put on hold will take years to compile, but here's an inkling: more than $200 million in insurance claims has already been paid out, and the numbers are still climbing. And, by the time the worst was over, more than 50,000 people had been evacuated from their homes. Of those, 334 families returned to find everything destroyed.

Statistics can also be misleading. There were 2,511 fires recorded in 2003, only slightly more than the annual statistical average of 2,500 and far short of the 1994 provincial record of 4,011. Obviously, the true measure of 2003's 2,511 fires is more

FACING PAGE: Captain Brian
Roach in the Operation Peregrine
logistics centre in Edmonton.
Shaughn Butts/the Edmonton Journal

BELOW: Kelowna residents
Wes Pederson, wife Charlotte,
son Joel and daughter Karly clear
undergrowth as fires from nearby
Okanagan Mountain Park
threaten their property, August 21.
Richard Lam/Canadian Press

accurately taken by analyzing size and impact. The fires of 1994, for example, consumed almost 30,000 hectares, the fires of 2003 more than 266,000. Ten businesses were also destroyed.

One of these, the Tolko sawmill in Louis Creek, employed nearly 200 salaried workers. When some 72 homes were destroyed in the McLure-Barriere region, this, coupled with the loss of the local sawmill and the decision of the company not to rebuild, threatened to suck much of the economic life out of Louis Creek and the nearby town of Barriere. Yet in the months since the fire, the blue-collar communities of the North Thompson—Louis Creek, Barriere, McLure and Heffley Creek—have shown a resilience and determination to regenerate. How successful these efforts will be remains to be seen.

THERE CAN BE FEW SIGHTS more terrifying than a raging wildfire, but, according to the botanical and archaeological evidence, these infernos have long played a prominent role in British Columbia's natural and human history. In Canada's most westerly province, nature has crumpled the landscape between the Pacific Ocean and the Rockies into myriad geographical landscapes and microclimates. In its coastal regions, wildfires visit infrequently. But in the central and southern interior of the province, large-scale fires are part of the natural order.

It makes sense. When summer comes, so do wind and lightning. This weather, combined with the dry forests of the Kootenays, the Okanagan and the North Thompson, makes for flint and steel. But while the forest ecosystems of these regions have adapted to the ebb and flow of wildfires, humans have thrown off this delicate balance between survival and destruction. Now there are matches, downed power lines and sparks from grinding machinery in the equation. One of the fires of 2003, for example, at Vaseux

Mars water bomber drops
a load of water on a forest fire
just a few kilometres from
Osoyoos on July 17, 2003.
S. Paul Varga/the Penticton Herald

Lake south of Penticton, was attributed to a downed power line igniting the parched grass below; when the forests are tinder dry, it doesn't take much to set them alight. The British Columbia Forest Service has a term for this collision between man and wildfire. At briefing after briefing in the summer of 2003, parks officials referred to "interface fires" when describing a blaze on a community's outskirts.

IN 1886, ONE OF the province's first interface fires destroyed much of the then-frontier town of Vancouver. The blaze began shortly after 2 PM on a balmy June 13, when a sudden squall off English Bay stoked a slash burn west of Cambie Street. The inferno raced along the city's wooden sidewalks faster than a man could run, leaping from building to building with flames that reached upward more than 30 metres. At that time Vancouver was a community perched on the edge of a forest— much as Barriere and Louis Creek are today. And, at that time, the sky above Vancouver would have carried the same permanent haze from the burning of scrub and debris and trees felled on the community's borders. All told, some 400 buildings were destroyed. The *Encyclopedia of British Columbia*, published by Howard White, cites at least eight people killed, though eyewitness accounts describe dozens of deaths. With the city choked with anonymous drifters seeking work on the frontier, a comprehensive tally of victims could never be completed.

A classic early days interface fire also took out much of the east Kootenay community of Fernie, first in 1904 and then, more drastically, in 1908. This fire shared many of the characteristics of the Vancouver blaze. It took place on August 1, another hot summer's day. It, too, began in logging slash, jumped into a pine forest and from there into a town of wooden buildings. Eighteen people of a community of 5,000 were killed and 1,000 buildings destroyed in little more than 90 minutes. The flames were so intense they melted cars parked in the street. Far more residents would have died had not local coal miners, skilled in rescue, taken charge of the evacuation. They shepherded terrified townsfolk to the railway station and onto rolling stock cars, which carried the residents to safety through the blazing town. Those who couldn't be evacuated were jammed for safety into the town's only stone structure.

"What impressed me

was the courage of the people

that I met."

PRIME MINISTER JEAN CHRÉTIEN,

August 24, 2003, in Kelowna

BELOW: Pilot Eric Ebert.
Family handout

FACING PAGE, LEFT: Pilot Ian
Mackay. *Family handout*

FACING PAGE, RIGHT: Helicopter
pilot Ben von Hardenberg of Mission, B.C., was killed after his
helicopter crashed near 100 Mile
House while fighting a forest fire.
Family handout

Vancouver Island, too, has had its fair share of major fires. On July 6, 1922, Merville, a town near Courtenay built by soldiers returning from World War I, was destroyed by a massive forest fire. The pattern was familiar. A hot, dry wind, a summer's day and a smouldering fire that suddenly flared, leading to flames that one witness described as "jumping through trees half-a-mile at a time." As the flames consumed oxygen, they created their own wind, driving the blaze through the bush and quickly overrunning fire crews that had little option but to drop tools and run. On July 14, 1938, an even larger blaze began in a stack of logs near Campbell River, nicknamed "The Big Fire." By the time it had burned itself out, this whopper had consumed hundreds of kilometres of land stretching back to Courtenay.

B.C.'s modern era has also seen its share of destruction. In 1958, 3,039 fires destroyed a staggering 856,000 hectares of B.C. forest. In 1970, more than 4,000 fires were noted, a record narrowly beaten in 1994. In 1985, the bar was raised even further when 3,603 fires destroyed 236,000 hectares and cost $125 million to fight—much of the damage occurring in the Canal Flats area near Cranbrook. In 1994, Jeremy Kraiger, 19, the son of a Penticton firefighter, deliberately lit the Garnet fire in Alice Creek canyon. When it was done, the blaze had ripped through 18 homes, levelled 14,000 hectares of forest and cost $5.5 million to extinguish. (The disaster was much on the minds of Naramata residents threatened in the summer of 2003 by the southern flank of the Okanagan Mountain Park fire.) In 1998, Salmon Arm found itself under siege from the Silver Creek fire, which destroyed 16 homes and 25 farm structures, forced the evacuation of 7,500 people and consumed 6,300 hectares—the most ferocious of a season that recorded 2,665 fires. That year also saw a new record set for provincial expenditures on firefighting: $154 million. More recently, the number of annual forest fires hovered between a high of 1,781 in 2002 to a low of 1,207 in 1999.

IN PART, THE PROBLEM has always been that the province's communities are pushing ever farther into the forests, increasing the risk of interface fires. And the fires usually win. A forest fire in full flight voraciously consumes fuel, oxygen and heat, creating its own maelstrom through convection currents that drive hot air up and away. Tongues of fire can jump hundreds of metres across the forest canopy; at the right temperature, trees virtually explode into flames. Faced with such a force of nature, there was little early firefighters could do except try to extinguish a fire quickly and, if these efforts proved unsuccessful, try to get everyone out of the inferno's path. But the science of firefighting has changed since World War II. The mechanical boom driven by war resulted in improvements in airplanes and machinery. Better firefighting strategies were developed and coordination improved. As a result, B.C.'s firefighters have become better at extinguishing forest fires more quickly.

Yet scientists have increasingly realized that improved firefighting methods are interfering with Mother Nature. By allowing forest undergrowth to build up in greater amounts than would normally occur, when a fire does take hold the consequences are likely to be far more severe than if a forest had been allowed to burn according to nature's sporadic fire schedule. British Columbia's unique biological diversity includes many species of forests, each with its own individual fire profile. If humans don't interfere, some of the province's rainforests may not catch fire for hundreds of years, while in the Interior regions devastated in 2003, substantial forest fires would occur every five to 10 years, on average.

In the Interior's forests of Douglas fir and ponderosa pine, fire is a natural cleansing force that sweeps away undergrowth, renews grasses, releases seeds and generally revitalizes the forest. The cycle is so regular that fires are seldom severe enough to burn the trees themselves. But as John Betts, a forester with the Western Silvercultural Contractors Association, explains, decades of successfully fighting forest fires has created an unnatural forest, one thick with undergrowth and carpeted with generations of dead pine needles. The result is kindling, and when a fire does take hold, it does so with an unnatural ferocity, consuming trees it might otherwise have left unscathed and destroying healthy bacteria in the soils of the forest floor that nourish life. "The forest systems are out of whack due to our well-intentioned conservation practices, which dictate not letting the forests go up in smoke," says Betts. "The true root of the problem is the long-term denial of fire's rightful place in the forest."

Thus were the forests primed for the fire season of 2003.

"They are the heroes of this town.

This was what you call a hellfire. They stood

their ground and they saved this town."

JOHN McDERMOTT, a provincial emergency

program volunteer, referring to the local RCMP and volunteer

firefighters battling the Barriere fire

KAMLOOPS & AREA

McLURE, BARRIERE,

LOUIS CREEK, McGILLIVRAY

No ONE IS QUITE SURE exactly how it began, but a cigarette, a pile of tinder-dry cedar needles and a long hot summer all played a part.

Mike Barre says he started it. The McLure volunteer firefighter readily admitted as much to the B.C. Ministry of Forests fire inspector who interviewed him on the evening of July 30, 2003. "I told him the first night of the fire that I did it," said Barre, 50. "I feel terrible, beyond what words could say." He acknowledged that the fire began with a discarded cigarette but that "it was an accident."

Barre's neighbour, Cheryl Land, was the second person to learn of the fire when she saw the unemployed former prison guard racing down the street, yelling that he had started a fire. Smoke was already billowing from a 10-centimetre-deep bed of cedar needles behind the Barre and Land homes. The properties back onto a forested mountain overlooking McLure, a sprawling community of 285 people about 40 kilometres north of Kamloops. Land's husband, Chris, rushed up the hill with a shovel to smother the flames with dirt. But in minutes, it was already too late; the fire was too fierce for anyone to get close enough to battle it. And the McLure-Barriere fire was born.

Fire crews put in a fire guard (generally a trench dug with a bulldozer) to contain the blaze, but by July 31, flames had jumped over the barrier into heavy timber, firing sparks 300 metres ahead. By that evening, more than 30 homes had been

FACING PAGE: Aerial bombers attack this sudden fire on Mount Paul, on the northern edge of Kamloops. The fire sprang up mid-afternoon and was running wild within 30 minutes. *Stuart Davis/ the Vancouver Sun*

BELOW: Premier Gordon
Campbell walks along a ridge
above Kamloops August 5,
as a massive plume of smoke
from the Strawberry Hill forest
fire rises behind. *Ian Smith/
the Vancouver Sun*

evacuated, northward to Louis Creek and southward to Kamloops. A day later, Kamloops Fire Centre manager Dennis Gaudry tried putting the fire in context. "This fire is off the scale. It has become too dangerous to fight"—a firestorm fuelled by high winds and the convection currents it had created. In its first 24 hours, explained Gaudry, the inferno had already covered 12 kilometres and consumed more than 4,000 hectares, including blazing a path through the town of Louis Creek before it swept northward alongside the North Thompson River to the southern end of Barriere.

An evacuation order was issued to all 2,800 residents of the McLure-Barriere corridor, though a few souls held on as long as they could as the flames moved closer amidst a thick plume of rolling smoke. The word was soon out that 30 homes in McLure had been destroyed, and a string of flaming buildings marked the route north toward Barriere up Highway 5. As night drew near on July 31, one witness described the entire hillside as bathed in an orange glow. The village of Louis Creek and the Tolko sawmill were the first in the fire's path. Just beyond lay the larger town of Barriere.

Tolko mill manager Vern Parkstrom fought on with a skeleton crew until midday, August 1. He had a helicopter and a water bucket ready, but as the flames climbed the ridge behind the mill and swept across piles of lumber, the site was abandoned. Throughout that afternoon, a long convoy of vehicles began to stretch westward along the highway from Barriere to Little Fort: trucks and trailers stuffed with hastily gathered personal treasures and pets.

In Barriere, another line of vehicles lined the block by Ed Tenzer's Super Save Gas Station. With the power to the entire community cut, it was the only business still open, its pumps powered by a portable gas generator. Each customer was limited to $20 worth of gas, enough to get out of town. Trisha Gjestrum was one of those patiently waiting in line, her three dogs and one

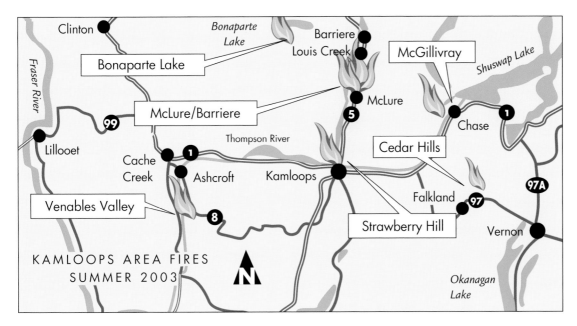

Clinton

Bonaparte
Lake

Barriere

Louis Creek

McGillivray

Shuswap Lake

Bonaparte Lake

Fraser River

McLure/Barriere

McLure

99

5

Chase

1

Thompson River

Lillooet

Cedar Hills

1

Cache
Creek

Ashcroft

Kamloops

97A

Venables Valley

8

Falkland

97

Strawberry Hill

Vernon

KAMLOOPS AREA FIRES
SUMMER 2003

N

Okanagan
Lake

parrot stuffed into the back of her small car. "I'm scared," she said. "But I've got the most important things right here with me."

Every new customer pulled up with a fresh rumour about the fire's advance. And as the smoke billowed overhead, enough was enough. "We've got to stop the pumps now," Cheryl Tenzer urged her husband. "Losing our lives isn't worth it."

Some stayed for a little longer. At the southern end of Barriere, Darcy Feller trained sprinklers on his roof and lawn. As he and local reporter Robert Koopmans watched the advancing smoke, Feller still held out hope he could keep the flying embers at bay. "It may not be a bad idea to stay here, to put out the spot fires," he told Koopmans. Then came the loud boom of propane tanks exploding in the Tolko yard. "I'll be okay," a shaken Feller said. "I don't know about my home."

As firefighters poured into the area, the first evacuees were gathering in an emergency reception centre in Kamloops. All residents were interviewed, asked their needs and assigned a place to live if they were unable to stay with family or friends. Tom and Marilyn Glanville of Barriere looked stunned and depressed as they arrived at the centre, set up in the Kamloops Sport Mart Place. "We had pigs, horses and cows, but we had no time to get them out," said Tom. "We could see it coming last night. Nothing like this has ever happened here before."

He was right. The McLure-Barriere fire would burn for almost two months before officials considered it sufficiently contained to stop issuing bulletins. And the fire still burned on into late fall, smouldering in the roots of trees in the forest. All told, it was one of the worst fires of the summer, consuming more than 26,000 hectares; incredibly, the worst of the damage occurred in the first four days.

ABOVE: Barriere/Louis Creek area forest fire on August 1, 2003. *Steve Grimaldi/B.C. Forest Service*

FACING PAGE: Smoke forms a giant cloud over Mount Paul as the Strawberry Hill fire picks up in the late afternoon near Kamloops. *Chuck Stoody/Canadian Press*

WHILE THE KAMLOOPS-AREA McLure-Barriere fire was the most significant indicator for many British Columbians that the province's wildfires were running out of control, B.C.'s firefighters were already well into the thick of things. In fact, by the time Mike Barre dropped his cigarette, three of B.C.'s largest fires were already burning. Two had come and gone. The Tatla Lake fire in the Cariboo had begun two weeks earlier, on July 18, and quickly spread with the help of erratic winds and dry forest underbrush. Residents of Alexis Creek were temporarily evacuated as the 2,400-hectare fire approached. Fortunately the series of fires throughout B.C. was already drawing reinforcements from as far away as New Brunswick. And by July 22, the Tatla fire was contained. Two days later, a smaller fire broke out near Sicamous, but a speedy attack by five helicopters and some 100 firefighters took the 100-hectare blaze down within five days.

Elsewhere, one of the largest fires of the year was still raging northeast of Chilko Lake in the Chilcotin. Starting July 22, that inferno burned for 20 days before being fully contained, but not before it had destroyed 29,200 hectares. Strong winds swelled the blaze, at one point bringing the flames within two kilometres of local homes. Firefighters, supported by water tenders and bulldozers, worked feverishly through the night to build fire guards. The huge fire stubbornly resisted. Over the coming weeks it would shift, propelled by strong winds, and in the town of Williams Lake, some 300 kilometres away, residents could already smell the smoke. On August 7, a trace of moisture and cooler winds provided some hope that the worst was over. By August 10, the Chilko Lake fire was under control.

Meanwhile, the 2003 firestorm was wreaking its worst havoc in the North Thompson. There were certainly more evacuees and more homes destroyed in the Kelowna region fires, but in some ways the residents of Louis Creek and Barriere—along with several more communities in the North Thompson—had much more to lose. The region is a less affluent area than the Kelowna district, and many of its burned-out homeowners lacked insurance. In fact, half of the first 150 to register at emergency evacuation centres admitted to having none.

ABOVE: Taking a break from fighting the Cedar Hills fire, Ryan Felix of Spallumcheen and his crew rest in the back of a pickup truck beside Highway 97. *Ian Smith/the Vancouver Sun*

RIGHT: Barriere volunteer fire department chief Al Kirkwood. *Ian Smith/ the Vancouver Sun*

FACING PAGE: Dustin Stenhouse, 11, stands in the remains of his former bedroom in the home his family moved from two years ago. The Stenhouse family took pictures of the home (near Highway 97), destroyed by the Cedar Hills fire. *Ian Smith/the Vancouver Sun*

"I just couldn't believe this place

burned down. The first time I heard it,

I just didn't believe it."

DUSTIN STENHOUSE, 11,

whose former Falkland home burned down

Times were tough in the region even before the fires. Up to a decade earlier, the valley had been prosperous, full of timber mills, but with the consolidation of the lumber industry many had closed. One indicator of the degree of hardship was the Barriere District food bank, whose president wearily commented in October 2003 that "we were feeding 300 people a month before the fire. Now we're feeding 1,600 a month."

The toughest blow of all was the loss of the Tolko mill, the region's largest employer and the source of its highest wages. The mill employed almost 200 people directly and was the lifeblood of dozens of independent contractors. Tolko had only purchased the Louis Creek operation in 1987, but a mill had operated in the village for more than 50 years.

AFTER THE FIRST FEW DAYS of frantic evacuations, a clearer picture emerged of the devastation along the North Thompson Valley. Already, the evacuation total had climbed to 5,000—half the valley's population, though Barriere itself had been largely saved from the flames, partly through the work of firefighters but also thanks to the volunteers who stayed to battle the fire. Although four businesses in the town's industrial section were destroyed, within the town limits no homes were lost. Barriere's volunteer fire chief Al Kirkwood—one of a team of more than 25 firefighters caught in the wildfire's midst—later described the scene: "We were surrounded by fire at one point. In fact, a crew from forestry was behind us with one of our trucks and they were trapped. They had fire behind them and fire in front of them. I had a crew from Clearwater in front of me and we drove through a firestorm to get out to try to save our own ass."

An emotional Steve Grimaldi of the B.C. Forest Service struggled to keep his composure as he described the experience. "It was a wild time, I can tell you that. When you see walls of fire 200 to 500 feet high coming down the valley . . . we did everything we could." John McDermott, a provincial emergency program volunteer, also described the scene. "They are the heroes of this town," he said of the local RCMP and volunteer firefighters. "This was what you call a hellfire. But they stood their ground and they saved this town."

FACING PAGE: Cpl. Federico Angulo, one of about 400 reservists with the B.C. regiment, exposes a "hot spot" with a pulaski tool as part of Operation Peregrine. Reserves from across Western Canada helped stabilize forest fire situations, attended to hot spots and provided camp and logistical support. *M.Cpl. Eric Jacques/Canadian Forces Garrison/ Edmonton Imaging*

ABOVE: Kamloops Fire Centre dispatcher Elaine Biffert directs air and ground crews to various fires as they flare up in the Kamloops fire district on Wednesday, August 6, 2003. Hundreds of forest fires were burning in the Kamloops region, and forest service workers, such as Biffert, were showing signs of fatigue. *Jason Payne/the Province*

ABOVE: At a morning media briefing on the state of the forest fires on August 4, Denis Gaudry, manager of the Kamloops Fire Centre, speaks in front of a map of the area. *Ian Smith/the Vancouver Sun*

Reporter Koopmans eloquently described the destruction at the Tolko mill. "Smoke continues to rise from the log piles and buildings," he wrote. "Heavy equipment parked out front shows evidence of the fierce heat, with rubber tires melted and windows gone. The remnants of several homes are evident along two kilometres southwest of Louis Creek. At one property, a tall brick chimney, a concrete foundation and a few burned-out cars are the only evidence a home once stood [there]. Yet in the midst of the destruction, there are surprises—odd sights that show the blaze had an arbitrary nature. There are many houses still standing in places where it seems they should not have been spared. Next to a house razed to the ground is another, almost unscathed. Some houses seem to have totally escaped—even the trees around the decks and porches are lush, while underbrush just a metre away is burned."

B.C. premier Gordon Campbell flew over the destruction on August 5, landing briefly to talk to firefighters. Three days earlier he had declared a state of emergency in the Thompson-Nicola Regional District, the first since the Salmon Arm fires of 1998. "It's just like a nuclear bomb went off . . . it's horrible to see," said a shaken Campbell. "The mill obviously was just a raging inferno."

The arbitrary nature of the fires' destruction would become a major theme of the media coverage, yet emergency officials' handling of this information became a bone of contention, not only to reporters but to residents. Provincial officials ordered reporters and photographers not to take pictures of destroyed homes, on the grounds that the images would upset residents. The media were also barred from evacuation centres set up in Kamloops, Vernon, Salmon Arm and 100 Mile House. Officials also withheld specific information on the extent of the fires' damage, even arresting one television reporter who attempted to enter an evacuated area with an animal rescue team. But the news blackout had the opposite effect on the public. The fickle nature of the McLure-Barriere fire led some to hope their homes had

ABOVE: Steve Grimaldi of the B.C. Forest Service Protection Branch outside the forestry office in Kamloops, with some of the equipment he uses to investigate the cause of forest fires. *Jason Payne/the Province*

LEFT: Angry Barriere resident Ray McDonald shows up at a media briefing in Kamloops August 4 to vent his fury that information about which homes have been destroyed is not being made available. *Ian Smith/the Vancouver Sun*

BELOW: An aircraft dumps fire
retardant August 2 on the steep slope
of Mount Paul to stop one of three
forest fires in the area from advancing. *Chuck Stoody/Canadian Press*

been spared, and the wait for information was unbearable. Barriere resident Ray McDonald vented his frustration at a community meeting, where he stood up and angrily harangued the podium. "I want to go home," demanded McDonald. "I want to know what's going on. I want to see."

In the coming month, officials seemed to have gotten the message. By the time the Kelowna fire peaked, reporters and photographers were allowed to cross the fire lines to tell the stories of the heroes fighting the blaze and to show the effects of the fire—images that heightened the impact on the public. British Columbians looked into their hearts, fuelling a wave of empathy and a flood of donations. And by the time the first evacuees of the McLure-Barriere fire pulled into Kamloops, help was ready. As they registered at the emergency response centre, every individual was offered food, clothing and a place to stay. Local businesses, particularly concerned about the trauma experienced by children, flooded the centre with Kleenex and stuffed toys. Over the coming weeks, Kamloops-

ABOVE: At the Puhallo Ranch, Pete Puhallo, Steve Puhallo and Chris Rice watch the fire across the Thompson River. *Mike Eng/the Province*

area residents threw open their homes, and businesses of every type contributed money and products to help ease the burden on evacuees. More than 2,000 in the community contacted various aid agencies to volunteer their help. Funding efforts were also deluged with support, money raised from a myriad of events—from pancake breakfasts to benefit pool contests. The Salvation Army and the Mennonite Disaster Service also collected for the evacuees. And Kamloops car dealer George Evans set up the North Thompson Relief fund, with an initial target of $200,000. By mid-October, the fund had raised more than $2 million.

The money would go toward any expenses people might have that weren't covered by government or insurance companies, said Evans—everything from prescription glasses to precision tools. "Our funds are going to be used not only to rebuild homes but also to stabilize the economy in Barriere as best we can," he said. "Our role is to help people rebuild their lives."

RIGHT: An empty road runs through a burned section of Strawberry Hill in Kamloops, August 5. The Strawberry Hill fire was one of three in the area that caused the evacuation of nearly 4,000 residents.
Richard Lam/Canadian Press

ABOVE: Debris from a burned-out section of Louis Creek, north of Kamloops, seen from the air on August 5. Residents were evacuated when the fire moved in from McLure-Barriere. *Richard Lam/ Canadian Press*

FACING PAGE: Firefighters hose down a house in McLure. *Steve Grimaldi/B.C. Forest Service*

As the fire raged on, health-care emergency officials prepared for the worst. Patients at the Royal Inland Hospital in Kamloops were moved to make way for those who might be injured in the fire. Luckily, there were few, though one man who was badly burned protecting his home was treated and transferred to the Vancouver General Hospital's burn unit. Thick air pollution was quickly identified as the major health hazard. Within the first few days of August, the air around Kamloops carried smoke from three major fires at McLure-Barriere, Strawberry Hill and Cedar Hills/Falkland. Two Barriere doctors, Terry Clare and Douglas Jack, set up shop in a Kamloops walk-in clinic. "There are lots of people from Barriere and the surrounding areas who have been displaced, and they still need medical services," said Clare. "It's reassuring for the people . . . especially the elderly, to phone in and get a familiar voice and see a familiar face."

Provision was also made for the hundreds of animals that had to be abandoned in the dash for safety. Within a week of the McLure-Barriere fire's outbreak, the Society for the Prevention of Cruelty to Animals had collected more than 400 cats and dogs at its Kamloops shelter and rescued about 200 horses, cows, sheep and other livestock.

BY AUGUST 8, the public outcry for information and the efforts of firefighters enabled many evacuees to begin returning home. But the situation remained uncertain as winds gusting up to 80 kilometres per hour pushed the fire in one direction and then another. The twin hazards of dry ground and lightning remained ever present.

Cecil Hay, 75, was one of the unlucky ones when he returned home. His Louis Creek trailer was destroyed and he lost dozens of tools. He was taking a rest from the heart-breaking task of sifting through the charred remnants when he was interviewed, sipping coffee by a Salvation Army truck. "A lot of that stuff we've had for 40

years," said Hay. "[My wife and I] both lost our wedding rings and all the stuff we got for our 25th anniversary. "I don't know what we're going to do. I'm just glad Barriere was saved, or there would be 200 or 300 people feeling like I do right now."

Still, residents were in a forgiving mood, even to the man who had accidentally started the fire. "The first day, there was a lot of hatred," says Cheryl Land. At first, she herself says she was angry but on reflection realized "it was a mistake."

Stu Geoghegan of Louis Creek, whose home and trailer park were destroyed, was also willing to turn the other cheek. "I told him it was a stupid thing to do," says Geoghegan. "But there's no sense in feeling bad about him."

Businesses in the area were also counting the costs. While few had been burned to the ground, the closure of access roads and the absence of the summer's tourists were hitting hard. Sun Peaks Resort north of Kamloops, for example, cut off by the threat of the Strawberry Hill fire and closure of the Yellowhead Highway, lost between $60,000 and $80,000 a day after guests were asked to leave. An air of uncertainty hung over the entire region's tourist industry. The smoke, combined with the newspaper headlines, had driven away most of the area's $40 million annual tourist trade, even from places not affected by the flames. The lumber industry suffered, too. Fallers were staying out of the forests, either to avoid the fires or to prevent accidentally starting new ones. Log prices rose, sawmills shut, and workers were laid off.

The media's images of the immense firefighting effort told only part of the story. British Columbians could see the fire engines and the exhausted firefighters catching a few hours' rest between shifts. But behind those images was an immense firefighting machine, from weather forecasters who constantly issued bulletins on wind and temperature to volunteers on the fire line, dampening hot spots with portable hoses and shovels. The first in the line of defence were the forecasters, mapping the lightning storms and shifting winds. Dozens of pilots were involved in ongoing aerial assaults, beginning with reconnaissance missions after every thunderstorm, to determine whether new fires had started. With new fires starting sometimes dozens at a time, decisions had to be made on which ones were top priority.

FACING PAGE: Barriere is devastated by a forest fire—a power pole felled by the flames causes blackouts in the area. *Ian Smith/ the Vancouver Sun*

BELOW: The Tolko sawmill in Louis Creek lies completely destroyed. *Ian Smith/the Vancouver Sun*

ABOVE: George Evans, owner of River City Nissan in Kamloops and the man behind the North Thompson Relief Fund, which raised more than $2 million to help fire victims. *Brendan Halper/the Vancouver Sun*

The call would then go out to the "bird dogs," spotter planes that call in the water bombers and helicopters. If a fire can be hit quickly from the air, it can be put out before it spreads. If possible, an initial attack could also be carried out by crews flown in by helicopter; a staging area would be cut and water ferried in. When a fire took hold, the tactics changed. The philosophy became: Whenever possible, allow a fire to consume itself by surrounding it with fire guards while patrolling its exteriors to douse spot fires. The biggest threat to the firefighters were the combustible undergrowth and the wind, which threw embers hundreds of metres through the treetops. When a fire approached a home, a crew of structural firefighters would stand its ground for as long as possible, dousing roofs and flammable undergrowth with water and fire retardant. Fixed-wing water bombers and helicopters would also dive-bomb the site. In these situations, with homes at stake, firefighters would fight to stay until the flames were on top of them, and sometimes around them.

Every day, the perimeters of the fires were patrolled. If the flames jumped a fire guard, another was built. These guards were physical barriers, carved through the forest with bulldozers—mostly by hundreds of volunteer loggers. Another technique was the controlled burn, carried out in front of the flames to burn off the brush and grass the fire needed for fuel. Once stationary, a fire would burn itself out.

As the flames died down, fire crews began the tough work of mopping up. Flames can burn into a tree's roots and travel underground—hot spots that can smoulder for months then burst into life with a gust of wind. Working in grid patterns, firefighters combed the ground and concentrated on any smoking areas, which they doused with hoses linked to portable water tanks. Sometimes crews would "cold trail" by digging into the ground with their bare hands to feel for hot spots. The mop-ups were a gradual progression, with workers shifting steadily inward from the perimeter to the centre of each dying fire. As they moved inward, a wary eye was kept open for escape routes. A blast of wind in the wrong direction, and a stationary fire can turn deadly.

BELOW: Relief volunteers unload a truck full of water and cleaning supplies, including mops and plastic garbage bags, at a relief centre in Barriere, August 9. *Chuck Stoody/ Canadian Press*

BELOW: Pte. Tracy Scott of the Princess Patricia's Canadian Light Infantry, centre, and Cpl. Chris Krafchek, right, hit hot spots while working on the McLure-Barriere fire on August 28. *Murray Mitchell/ the Province*

FACING PAGE: Kamloops-area forest fire. *Steve Grimaldi/ B.C. Forest Service*

BY MID-AUGUST, cooler weather was offering a welcome respite for firefighters. The McLure-Barriere fire had already affected almost 20,000 hectares, but two other fires in the North Thompson area, at Strawberry Hill and Cedar Hills, had been contained. The Strawberry Hill fire was a major concern during the first two weeks of August. At one point, some 4,000 residents were driven from suburbs in northern Kamloops, including Rayleigh and Heffley Creek. They were back in their homes by August 9; that no homes were lost was due to the heroic efforts of firefighters. The Strawberry Hill fire destroyed some 5,731 hectares; Cedar Hills, 1,620. Yet despite its relatively small size, the Cedar Hills fire levied the heavier toll, especially on the community of Falkland some 60 kilometres southeast of Kamloops.

On August 6, 11-year-old Dustin Stenhouse examined the destruction of his former Falkland home with a mixture of disbelief and fascination. The ground-floor bedroom was a pile of charred and ashy remains around the mangled and blackened frame of a bed bunk. The circular skeleton of a trampoline sat beneath a row of blackened and rust-coloured pine trees; the twisted metalwork of the family camper van was splayed before a crisp, blackened field. "I just couldn't believe this place burnt down," says Stenhouse. "The first time I heard it, I just didn't believe it."

The Strawberry Hill fire was contained after 15 days thanks to the efforts of 245 firefighters. The Cedar Hills fire took 359 people and another 15 days to bring under control—with one unexpected consequence. A firefighter discovered the bones of a man who had been missing for nearly eight years. Police began a homicide investigation.

With fires burning throughout the province, Kamloops and the southeast region of B.C. were now in the eye of the storm. Almost 700 of the 878 fires then burning were located here, the most devastating being the McLure-Barriere blaze. Others included a 1,000-hectare inferno in Venables Valley south of Ashcroft, which came within 800 metres of that community's homes before being fended off. Some 60

FACING PAGE: Helicopters fill
their buckets with water to fight
Kamloops-area fires. *Mike Eng/
the Province*

people were evacuated but were able to return after a few days. By the time it was
finally contained in mid-September, by firefighters numbering up to 330 at a time,
the Venables fire had consumed 7,635 hectares. The McGillivray Lake-Niskonlith
Lake fire had also taken hold by mid-August, destroying 2,000 hectares. Triggered
by lightning, it would rapidly grow and within days threaten a number of communities, including Chase. And on the eastern shore of Lake Okanagan, a small blaze of
some 400 hectares was beginning to swell in Okanagan Mountain Park.

More than two weeks after it started, the McLure-Barriere fire showed it still
had teeth. Following a wind shift on August 16, 500 evacuation orders were issued
for residents north of Kamloops, some of whom had just returned to their homes.
Only one day later, on August 17, helicopter pilot Ben von Hardenberg, 33, died as
he lifted off from a staging area trailing a long line and bucket, then crashed. The
pilot had been fighting a fire near Bonaparte Lake east of 100 Mile House, which
had broken out August 6, apparently from a lightning strike. Konrad von Hardenberg says his younger brother was planning to marry his sweetheart within two
weeks and move to Brisbane, Australia. The youngest of six boys was killed on
his last day of duty for Gemini Helicopters of Grande Prairie. "When it comes to
fire season, pilots go wherever the need is greatest," says von Hardenberg. "Ben
had just finished a tour in Saskatchewan and in Ontario, then he had five days [in
B.C.]. Sunday was his last day."

RCMP initially ordered 15 homes evacuated, and crews trained in dampening
fires near residences moved in. The fire proved stubborn, with strong local winds
fanning flames over the fire guards. But by September 10, crews had contained the
fire within its 1,500-hectare borders.

Also in mid-August, as the McLure-Barriere fire retreated, firefighters' efforts
switched to the McGillivray fire south of Chase. On August 17, about 500 residents
were evacuated from this largely rural area, which includes the Adams Lake and
Niskonlith Lake Indian reserves. At one point, the fire came within three kilometres of Chase's boundaries. But one family stayed because they lacked insurance
on their newly built home on the shores of Niskonlith Lake and were able to give a
graphic account of their miraculous survival.

In all, 13 people were dampening buildings when the roaring flames approached. The makeshift fire crew had no option but to escape into the lake using two inner tubes, a canoe and a small fibreglass boat. "It was just wild, wild, wild, wild," said Robert Oakland. "Stuff was coming down on us out of the sky—it was like a hailstorm, there was so much of it—and you couldn't open your eyes it was so hot, and the smoke was just so thick you couldn't see a thing anyway, and there was so little oxygen it was hard to take a breath. The wind kicked up, and then the canoe tipped over and the boat got swamped, and everybody went in. At one point my wife [Debbie] was hanging on the bow of the sunken skiff and staying afloat by holding a Thermos bottle underneath her arm."

The Oaklands were rescued by a neighbour in an electric-powered boat, who pulled them into the middle of the lake. When the family returned home, they discovered that, while an old log cabin and outbuildings had burned, their new home still stood—only a little charred around the edges.

The day following the Oaklands' escape, the fire situation was no better. On some flanks, the McGillivray and Barriere fires burned where they stood, starved of fuel by controlled burns or through the pounding of the aerial assault. But in other places the fires jumped their guards; both grew some 500 hectares during the night. By August 19, 850 people had been evacuated from Pritchard. By August 23 they were allowed home, only to discover that at least two residences had been ransacked by looters. In a summer of so much community spirit, it was one of the lowest points. Still, as the fire season entered the final two weeks of August, the

FACING PAGE: Louis Creek
area home ablaze. *Steve Grimaldi/
B.C. Forest Service*

LEFT: A firefighter works on a
smouldering fire in the Kamloops
hills. *Stuart Davis/the Vancouver Sun*

fire crews seemed to be holding their own. There was still a flurry of evacuation alerts throughout the Kamloops region, but the news in B.C. Forest Service bulletins seemed more optimistic. Then on August 20, the government imposed a backcountry advisory for the whole of southern B.C., the most widespread in the province's history.

"We're concerned about the safety of the public out there . . . and we don't want any more human-caused fires," said government spokesman Rick Clevette. The same day, 340 troops from Edmonton arrived in Vernon for a crash course in firefighting. They were the most recent contingent of Operation Peregrine, the name given to the Canadian armed forces gathered from across the country. By the time these troops and reservists pulled out in mid-September, some 2,600 from every service branch of the Canadian armed forces had seen firefighting action. Their discipline made them ideal recruits for the dangers posed on the fire lines.

Fresh from the front, where he was attended by a medic who dug a wooden splinter from his hand, B.C. reservist Cpl. Federico Angulo spoke of the heady mix of fear, excitement and grim determination that infected his comrades. "Every time you see a tree candling in front of you, you get scared," said Angulo. "But you're going to fight it; you're going to knock it down. Everyone here is a volunteer—we all wanted to do it. Every day we're excited to go up there and do our part."

Capt. Dan Thomas of B.C.'s reserve force 39 Brigade Group put it in suitably military terms. "Calling it a war is a very appropriate analogy," said Thomas. "We are dealing with an unpredictable enemy who has the initiative."

By now almost 1,000 firefighters were tackling the McLure-Barriere fire, while the entire town of Chase remained on a one-hour evacuation alert. In Kamloops, a T-shirt proclaiming "You can't burn our spirit" went on sale as a relief fund-raiser. North of Kamloops, Kathy Bassett, 54, refused to evacuate from the McLure-Barriere fire in order to tend her sheep, cattle and goats. With her truck packed, she was determined to hang on until the last moment. "I'm watching. Anybody would be a fool not to be nervous . . . You have to laugh or else you go crazy." But Bassett also offered a simple message for Prime Minister Jean Chrétien. "Send more money," she said. "Send more water bombers."

BELOW: Photo taken by a senior fire investigator shows the intensity of a blaze in the Louis Creek area north of Kamloops, which forced the evacuation of homes. *Steve Grimaldi/B.C. Forest Service*

BELOW: The former home of
Louis Creek residents Stu and Ally
Geoghegan, destroyed by a fire in
August. The couple is currently
rebuilding. *Jason Payne/the Province*

ABOVE: Little remains of a home at Louis Creek after a forest fire swept through the area. *Chuck Stoody/Canadian Press*

THE DRY CONDITIONS in the Fraser Canyon, from Hope to Cache Creek, gave rise to one particularly quirky fire on August 21. A semi-truck collision near Hell's Gate sparked a fire on a steep hillside that quickly devoured 80 hectares. The fire was attacked aggressively, but at one point an evacuation alert was issued and, with the loss of power, the Hell's Gate Tramway was shut down. Debbie McKinney, the tramway's general manager, was frustrated by the daily loss of between $10,000 and $20,000. "This is hay season for us," said McKinney. "People spend lots of money to come to British Columbia and tour and visit, and to come up here and find out they can't take the tram ride . . . they're disappointed."

The fire, which eventually destroyed 144 hectares, was extinguished by August 27. By then, in Kamloops, the battle seemed to be turning. High winds predicted for the weekend of August 23 failed to materialize, allowing firefighters to reinforce their guards along the various fire edges with controlled burns. Eight hundred people in both the Barriere and Pritchard regions were given the all clear to go home. And Kamloops promised food and shelter for up to 5,000 evacuees to its fire-ravaged neighbour, Kelowna. Thankfully, the offer proved unnecessary.

On August 28, fire officials announced the McLure-Barriere fire was 75 per cent contained. The damage assessment that was released put the price tag at more than $8.2 million, with 163 structures burned, including homes and outbuildings. But support for the battered emergency workers continued to pour in, along with the latest contingent of registered massage therapists. "RMTs can help relieve some of the [emergency workers'] physical pain, reduce the high levels of stress they are experiencing and help keep them on the front lines," said spokeswoman Sandra Coldwell. "These people are saving lives and saving communities. We need to do everything we can to help them succeed."

On August 28, the government changed its backcountry advisory to an outright ban that stretched across southern B.C., from Vancouver Island to Alberta. Fines of up to $10,000 were threatened, with the ruling enforced until September 12. In the Sea-to-Sky corridor, more than two dozen people were ticketed for breaking its conditions. Those who went into the backcountry were fined $230; those who started campfires, $345 per offence. As August drew to an end, though, there was a feeling that the worst was over. The McLure-Barriere fire was 85 per cent contained, the McGillivray fire controlled by 75 per cent and the Venables fire by 50 per cent. The number of evacuees had shrunk from a high of 10,000 to 100. And on September 3, Jim McBride, director of community services for the Thompson-Nicola regional district, sounded a note of optimism. "We feel better," he said. "Things are beginning to wind down. There is light at the end of the tunnel . . . It would be nice to take this thing to the next step and give an all clear. But that's up to Kamloops fire control and the office of the fire commissioner."

Almost. The McGillivray fire was to put on one last show. On September 6, as a cold weather front moved in, the shifting winds accompanying it drove flames within three kilometres of Sun Peaks Resort. An evacuation order was issued and some 1,000 visitors, including a wedding party of 250, were forced to immediately pack and move out. It would be another six days before the order was lifted. By then, firefighting efforts were winding down, with ground forces shrinking to 3,500 from the 5,200 of a week before.

As the smoke cleared in mid-September, firefighters in the Kamloops area were exhausted. More than 750 fires had burned 106,570 hectares with a further 70,000 hectares consumed in the Cariboo and Prince George regions. Ten of the Kamloops fires were among the province's list of 23 most serious. And even when the threat of another wildfire was considered passed, more than 2,000 firefighters were still in the bush dampening stubborn blazes.

One forestry source estimates 56,000 man-hours were used to subdue the McGillivray blaze alone, and it wasn't even the largest. "These fires aren't fathomable," says forestry official Valerie Dettwiler. The human toll remains to be fully tallied. The fires drove some 10,000 residents throughout the Kamloops area from their homes. Some were evacuated several times, at the mercy of the whims of changing winds and flames in a torrid six weeks of an unforgettable summer.

ABOVE: A destroyed car in Louis Creek. *Jason Payne/the Province*

"It's just terrifying. I'm traumatized. The fire was in my backyard. I loved my home. It was my castle."

KIM ROBERTSON,

who lost her Kettle Valley home

KELOWNA & AREA

NARAMATA, OKANAGAN FALLS,

OSOYOOS, PENTICTON

THE BOLT OF LIGHTNING struck Squally Point, where the rugged southern Interior hillside juts like the bow of a ship toward Okanagan Lake, just after midnight on Saturday, August 16, 2003. The fire was spotted for the first time at 2:05 AM and reported by a woman who could see the flames from her Peachland home clear across the lake. The fire soon exploded, fuelled by ferocious westerly winds that were sliced in half when they hit the point, sending gusts north toward Kelowna and south to Penticton. "It's taken off to the north and south. It's a double-headed monster," was how local fire information officer Karen Cairns described it.

Little more than one hour after it was called in, the Okanagan Mountain Park blaze had grown to 10 hectares. By 6:18 AM, it was a Rank Five fire, the second-highest on the intensity scale used by fire officials. Air tankers, helicopters dropping massive buckets of water and an initial attack crew of 26 firefighters pounced on the inferno, beating it down to a Rank Two that same morning. There was a collective sigh of relief. The air tankers were redeployed to fight other large wildfires raging in B.C. But by 1 PM, the stubborn beast had roared back to life, frustrating the efforts of ground crews. Barely an hour later, the flames had grown so large they were burning through fire retardant sprayed on the forest, where the tops of trees ignited like candles. Every resource not being used on other fires burning in

FACING PAGE: A damaged but still-standing home is framed by a melted basketball hoop belonging to a destroyed home on Westridge in Kelowna's Crawford Estates subdivision. *Gerry Kahrmann/ the Province*

55

ABOVE: Flames from wildfires consume homes on a hillside of Kelowna late in the evening of August 22. *Andy Clark/Reuters 2003*

the province was thrown at the blaze, but it continued to grow. Daily, it burned steadily toward Kelowna, the largest city in the B.C. Interior with more than 100,000 residents.

As Kelowna grew through the 1990s, trendy suburbs of middle- and upper-class homes had been carved out of the local mountains, offering stunning views of Okanagan Lake against a backdrop of dense forest. That August weekend, curious residents gathered at the end of their driveways to watch the red glow approach. By Monday, as the blaze wiped out more than 1,000 hectares, they began to worry. The flames looked to be about six kilometres away. "As night fell, you could really see the glow intensify. By midnight, it had climbed up a ridge. We figured it travelled three kilometres or more in a two-hour period," recalls Lindsay McDonald, whose family lost three homes in the fire: his, his in-laws' and his sister-in-law's. "At that time, myself and my neighbours on either side knew we were in trouble."

By Tuesday, August 19, 100 residents had been ordered to leave their properties and 1,013 more were on evacuation alert as the fire devoured 2,800 hectares of forest left tinder dry by a rainless summer. With smoke clogging the air, homeowners removed burnt pine needles and ash from their lawns and put sprinklers on their houses. Some cut down trees or removed thick vegetation in an effort to stop the fire from spreading. "The hue of the red glow got brighter and brighter, and you just got this feeling that a big army is marching toward you and there's nothing you can do to stop it," recalls homeowner Ralf Pfob.

By Wednesday, the fire had grown to a massive 11,000 hectares, and Mervyn Andrews began to sense there was something very wrong in the hills above his family's Okaview Road home, on the edge of Kelowna. "There was an eerie stillness through the whole area," says the schoolteacher. "It was so quiet, and the birds were actually starting to blend into flocks as if it was fall and they were ready to migrate."

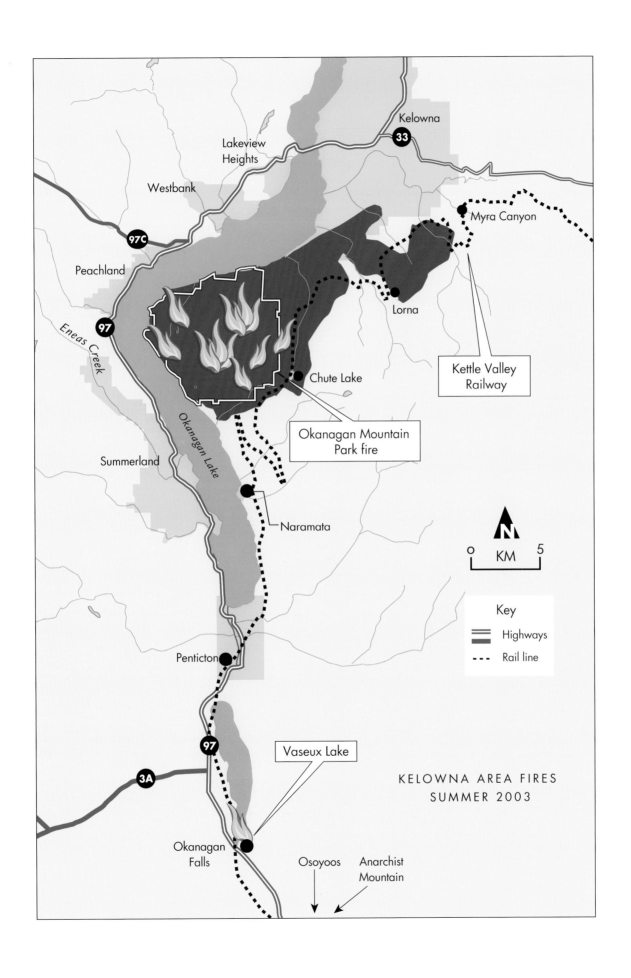

Kelowna

33

Lakeview
Heights

Westbank

Myra Canyon

97C

Peachland

Kettle Valley
Railway

Eneas Creek

97

Lorna

Chute Lake

Okanagan Mountain
Park fire

Okanagan Lake

Summerland

Naramata

N

0   5
    KM

Key

═══ Highways

--- Rail line

Penticton

Vaseux Lake

97

3A

KELOWNA AREA FIRES
SUMMER 2003

Okanagan
Falls

Osoyoos   Anarchist
           Mountain

BELOW: Residents watch the approaching flames in Kelowna on August 22. Police with bullhorns ordered 20,000 people from their homes in the southern suburbs as fast-moving flames moved closer.
Richard Lam/Canadian Press

"I don't know if we're ever

going to get it out."

BRIAN GLOVER, Vancouver firefighter,

referring to the Kelowna fires

Most residents had begun packing their valuables, particularly irreplaceable items such as photographs and scrapbooks. Others, flustered, grabbed odd things, such as the case of motor oil packed by Jim Stewart. Karen DesJardins was very thorough, emptying her Kelowna home of the furniture handcrafted by her husband, and most of her six-year-old son Barclay's toys.

At this point, 80 firefighters were battling the out-of-control blaze but couldn't stop it from burning through 95 per cent of Okanagan Mountain Provincial Park, a 10,000-hectare expanse known for its scenic lakes, bike trails and horseback riding. The inferno was fuelled by winds of up to 80 kilometres per hour, soaring temperatures that reached 40°C and a massive accumulation of branches and leaves on the forest floor. The fire was "beyond what we've ever seen before. There's absolutely nothing our crews or equipment or helicopters can do to stop a fire from spreading that fast," said Kevin Matuga of the B.C. Forest Service.

Bulldozers cleared wide paths of trees to create fire guards inside the forest, and containment lines were cut around the perimeter of some properties in the area, including the Cedar Creek winery. From over a nearby burning ridge, chunks of hard ash the size of ping-pong balls blew over the house of vintner Tom DiBello. "It looked like a nuclear explosion over there," was how DiBello put it.

Most of the community in south Kelowna was on evacuation alert, and by 7:45 PM Thursday, 5,000 residents were ordered to leave after flames broke through a fire guard just three kilometres beyond some 1,000 homes. Sirens echoed through the smoke as Mark Fleming fled his Kettle Valley subdivision home with his wife and two young daughters. "The flames were coming right at us," says Fleming, shuddering as he remembers.

Const. Robert Charron of the Kelowna RCMP knocked on doors to make sure everyone was out. "The majority of people were prepared and good to go," he says. "Ten per cent were in total disbelief

BELOW: Naramata resident Joann Pfeifer holds her favourite keepsake picture of her son, Randy, as she prepares to flee the Okanagan Mountain fire. *Steve Bosch/ the Vancouver Sun*

RIGHT: Flames and smoke move dangerously close to a residential area of Kelowna in the early hours of August 23. *Andy Clark/Reuters 2003*

BELOW: The news is good for some, devastating for others, when Kelowna residents learn at a meeting August 24 whether the forest fire has levelled their homes. *Ian Smith/the Vancouver Sun*

FACING PAGE: People affected by the evacuation in southern Kelowna line up at the Parkinson Recreation Centre to register for assistance. *Steve Bosch/the Vancouver Sun*

and there were two per cent in total denial. Thankfully, we eventually convinced them it was time to go."

The mass exodus caused a panicked traffic jam, and tensions ran high as drivers watched the approaching flames in their rear-view mirrors. Motorists fled to one of two evacuation centres set up at a local recreation centre and high school. That night, 15 houses, each valued at about $500,000, were destroyed. Smouldering hot spots, deep banks of ash and the skeletal remains of chimneys and concrete foundations were all that remained. "They are totally destroyed," Kelowna Fire Chief Gerry Zimmermann said. "There is no in-between. There is nothing left."

BATTLING THE WILDFIRES was particularly personal for three Kelowna firefighters who would also lose their homes during the ordeal. John Kelly reported for work just four hours after learning his house was gone. "I was trying to focus, but I had a real hard time. It was just disbelief and utter shock," says Kelly, though he doesn't blame his colleagues for not saving his property. "I want everyone to know that they did their best."

The loss of those first 15 houses in Kelowna grabbed the attention of politicians in Victoria and Ottawa, and federal defence minister John McCallum and B.C. premier Gordon Campbell toured the devastation the next day. "The forces of nature are incredible, and they are beyond my ability to describe," said Campbell.

By midday Friday, the fire had grown to 17,000 hectares—more than 40 times the size of Vancouver's Stanley Park—and was being fought by 600 firefighters from the B.C. Forest Service, the military and municipal departments across B.C. About 250 bulldozers, two dozen helicopters, water tankers and two giant Oshkosh fire trucks from Alberta were also battling the blaze. The fire crews struggled to build new containment lines, remove anything combustible from the ground and hose down houses. But as the wind picked up, there was an underlying fear that their efforts were for naught.

ABOVE: Kelowna fire chief Gerry Zimmermann and firefighters at the main fire hall. *Ian Smith/ the Vancouver Sun*

FACING PAGE, TOP: Firefighting helicopters drop fire retardant on Gallagher's Canyon in East Kelowna September 7. *Nick Procaylo/the Province*

FACING PAGE, BOTTOM: A water bomber about to fill up with water from Okanagan Lake. It is fighting the fires that threaten the Kettle Valley Railway trestles in Myra Canyon. *Brian Sprout/ the Vancouver Sun*

"We're worried about this wind right now. It's blowing up good," said Patrick Crane, a 27-year veteran of the Kelowna Fire Department. His words had an ominous sense of foreshadowing. As the day progressed, it became more and more dangerous for those on the front lines. Several Vancouver firefighters were trapped above Okaview Road by the 70-metre-high rolling inferno. "Some guys, they didn't think they were going to make it," says Vancouver firefighter Ed Pickett, who was in contact by radio with his colleagues at Okaview. "All of a sudden, the wind blew up and it was all around them and they couldn't get out. They called us on the cellphone. They said, 'Guys, we're going to die.'" The men drove through a wall of flames to escape, as lightning flashed overhead.

Kelowna firefighter Tracy Melnyk was also caught in the blaze as it swept over Okaview just after 3:15 PM. "Within seconds, we had trees exploding. The firestorm blew past us over the road and surrounded us." Melnyk and his crew dropped to the ground. "Everyone had their face in the grass, trying to get air," recalls his colleague, Shawn O'Reilly. After 30 years with the Kelowna Fire Department, O'Reilly believed he too was about to die.

"There was a real rumble, and it just flashed all around us and everything went orange, and then everything was on fire," he recalls. "I was terrified. Everyone was really scared. There was nowhere to go." After the fire rolled over them, the firefighters escaped—miraculously, without any serious injuries—by running through thick, burning bush.

As fire crews battled the ever-growing monster in the forest, officials in downtown Kelowna were making plans to order more than 25,000 more residents from their suburban homes. And at dusk on Friday, August 22, police yelling into bullhorns ordered everyone to go. "It was havoc," recalls Larry Friesen of the evening he huddled outside the reception centre with his wife and two teenage sons. "They banged on the door and said, 'You've got to get out.'"

Some residents stayed with friends, others were placed in hotels, still others slept in motorhomes parked in the lot of a large Kelowna shopping mall. In total,

LEFT: A person watches the Okanagan Mountain Park forest fire light up the night sky from Peachland on August 21. The fire moved north during the evening, forcing the evacuation of 1,000 homes and nearly 5,000 residents. *Richard Lam/Canadian Press*

BELOW: An air tanker drops fire retardant on Pinnacle Ridge in east Kelowna. *Nick Procaylo/the Province*

30,000 people were forced from their homes—about one-third of the city's population; it is believed to be the largest evacuation in the shortest period of time in Canada's history. Most, but not all, of the residents obeyed the evacuation orders. Peter Esovoloff stayed behind while his wife, daughter and neighbours fled their rural farms and orchards in south Kelowna. "I said I'm not going to leave this place. If it goes, I want to see it go. Especially when you build [your home] piece by piece . . . it's hard leaving a place when you've been here your whole life," says Esovoloff, 67. "[My wife] said, 'You're crazy.' But I didn't want to worry from downtown."

Late that night, Kelowna Fire Department Lieut. Al Chatham was working in the heart of the fire near Okaview Road, a street that was amongst the hardest hit. Here, sparks and smoke reduced visibility to about 10 metres, and barbecue propane tanks exploded all around him. Firefighters scrambled from house to house, where they were forced to make unimaginable choices, such as letting one home burn so they could save the next. "To watch it burn and let it burn is wrong in your psyche," says the veteran firefighter. "It was war. Everybody was fighting as hard as they could."

O'Reilly, Chatham's colleague, says there was no way to prepare for what they were faced with that night. "If it was a city block, we're trained for that. But how the hell do you train for something that's five miles long and moving 100 metres a minute?" Tears well in the eyes of the rugged firefighter when he recalls the homes he couldn't save. "There were signs up there, you know, 'Please save my home.' Million-dollar homes were collapsing in 20 minutes. We might be able to protect two homes at a time, three homes. Then we'd have to break and run ahead of the fire. This area got totally wiped out."

BY SOME ESTIMATES, the flames were 100 metres high and advancing at 120 kilometres per hour when they roared into south Kelowna on August 22, weaving an illogical path of destruction that would obliterate one home and leave the one next

FACING PAGE AND BELOW:
B.C. Forest Service firefighters
work in the pitch black night,
putting out hot spots. *Ian Smith/
the Vancouver Sun*

*"I heard many guys describe
it as a war zone, and that's the best
way to describe it."*

AL CHATHAM, Kelowna firefighter

FACING PAGE: The Canadian military fighting fires in Kelowna. *Glenn Baglo/the Vancouver Sun*

BELOW: Cpl. Bonnie Stefanov, left, and Cpl. Tracy Neid listen to descriptions of the dangers they face. *Glenn Baglo/the Vancouver Sun*

door untouched. The hellfire vapourized some 223 homes that day, in addition to the 15 of the night before. Later that night, Ed Pickett, who had visited New York on behalf of the Vancouver fire department after the 2001 terrorism attacks, was awestruck by the devastation. "We went to New York after 9/11, and this is pretty comparable," he said at the time. "It looked like land after a nuclear war. Total desolation . . . like a nuclear holocaust."

Homes were reduced to smoking craters as indiscriminate "fingers of fire" clawed through the area. The acrid smell of burning plastic hung heavily in the air. A stainless steel dishwasher, still containing dirty dishes, was the only recognizable item inside the soot-covered foundation of one house. Some garden gnomes, melted children's toys and bird feeders sat among the debris, desolate reminders that families once thrived on these ruined lots. South Kelowna evacuees awoke Saturday morning with a sense of dread but most didn't find out until a community meeting Sunday whether their home was one of the 238 houses lost. They were shown maps of the fire-ravaged areas: properties coloured white had survived; those shaded black were destroyed. The moods of those leaving the meeting ranged from jubilation to sorrow. "I've got a home," yelled Warren Saari, as he pumped his hands in the air. "I thought [my house] was gone. I felt like I was going to puke. Then I was searching the map and there it was!"

But Dennis Hostland had his worst fears confirmed. His family lost everything in the fire because they were driving to Vancouver when the evacuation order came down so had no chance to remove any valuables. "Everything was in there, with the exception of some photos," recalls the devastated man.

Again, despite tremendous grieving at the meeting, residents showed no animosity toward the fire crews that were unable to save their homes. Instead, they gave Kelowna's popular fire chief a standing ovation. Zimmermann was

ABOVE, RIGHT AND FACING PAGE:
Firefighters in action in the
Lakeshore Drive area of Kelowna
on Friday afternoon, August 22.
Nick Procaylo/the Province

"This wasn't a minor event. This was a natural disaster."

RON MATTIUSSI, director of the emergency

operations centre, Kelowna

grateful for the community's support and proud of his workers for protecting most of the houses. "We got hammered pretty good. These losses are staggering," he said. "But for every one that burned down, they probably saved two."

The exhausted, disappointed fire crews still faced many long days of battling the wildfire, and the city rallied around them by hauling beer, cards, flowers and goodies to the main Kelowna fire hall. Tony D'Andrea spent six hours cutting out 1.2-metre-tall white cardboard letters that spelled "Thank You Firefighters!" then erected them on nearby Dilworth Mountain. Within two hours, 100 people flocked to the hillside to write messages of support on the sign. "There's a lot of people who wanted to give a lot of thanks," said D'Andrea. The letters were later moved to the fire hall, where thousands signed them. One note, from Laurie C., said: "I wish you seven hours of uninterrupted sleep, food in your stomach and the comfort of knowing how much you are all valued, appreciated and respected for the work you are doing. May you be safe at all times."

Hundreds of well-wishers from across Canada, the U.S. and overseas wrote more heartfelt notes, on a Web site created by the B.C. Forest Service to collect messages for the firefighters. "We cannot thank enough those brave firefighters who helped save our house in Nunsti Park," wrote David Williams. "We thought for sure it had been lost along with everything else there, and found out yesterday that it had been saved, probably because your crew put a sprinkler system in place. My son is on the fire line with the Salish crew from Pemberton, and I know what it is like to work under these difficult conditions."

Fire Lieut. Tim Light said the community's backing boosted morale. "We've had a pretty tough four or five days here so the support is really uplifting for every single guy on the fire department," he said. Fire crews also left their own notes of gratitude. Evacuee Ken Fisher returned home to find a dry-erase board leaning against his car with a note from some Princess Patricia Canadian Light Infantry (PPCLI)

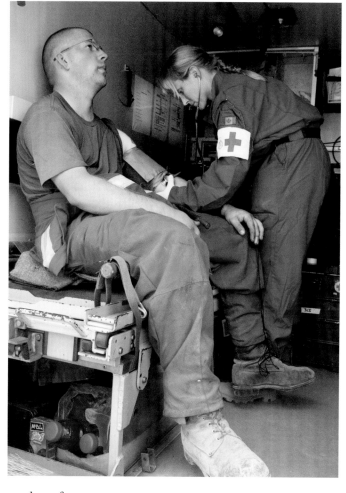

ABOVE: Cpl. Greg Pate receives care for heat exhaustion from medic Cpl. Ellen Amirault. *Glenn Baglo/ the Vancouver Sun*

FACING PAGE: Trooper Glenn Duffield, left, and Sgt. Sean Parker furiously build a fire break around an outburst of flames on a ridge outside Kelowna. *Glenn Baglo/ the Vancouver Sun*

RIGHT: Trooper Glenn Duffield takes a break from the dirty job of fighting fire. *Glenn Baglo/ the Vancouver Sun*

FACING PAGE: The end of another day for Cpl. Chris Marchetti. *Glenn Baglo/the Vancouver Sun*

soldiers who had taken refuge on his property while fighting the blaze: "Thanks for everything, from the soldiers of 1ppcli, Edmonton. Appreciate it deeply. We rested on your lawn at night. We tried to stop everything. Fire too powerful."

Fisher, whose Chute Lake Crescent house survived, was overwhelmed by the note. "It's been years since this old man cried," he says, "but that sign brought tears to my eyes. How the heck could they think to thank us for letting them sleep on the lawn?"

Winds died down that Sunday, and about 6,000 of the evacuees were allowed to return home. Beryl Itani, director of the city's emergency social services, helped the rest find accommodation, along with 90 goats, 237 dogs and 97 finches displaced by the fire. "We are getting businesses volunteering to help feed not only the people in the emergency operation centre and the staff at the reception centre, but also the evacuees," said Itani, a gentle, mother-hen type who has been doing the job for 20 years. "There's nothing like a disaster to bring a community together."

For every evacuee, there was frustration and inconvenience. Luis Calao had no suits to wear to work; mechanic Richard Shepherd had left behind his tools. "Oh man, I just want to get my life back to normal," said Gus Neilson, who camped with his wife and two teenagers after being evacuated. "I so miss the simple things, like having coffee in my backyard, reading the paper in the living room, watching my kids play on the swings—even to have a simple hot shower."

As Kelowna residents grappled with their changed lives, Prime Minister Jean Chrétien visited the city to shake the hands of evacuees and firefighters. "It is real devastation," Chrétien said, after flying over the 19,600-hectare fire that Sunday, August 24. "What impressed me was the courage of the people that I met. I know that they have lost their houses, or have just learned two minutes ago that they've lost their homes and so on, but the strength of the community was amazing."

ALTHOUGH THE WIND BLEW the flames of the Okanagan Mountain Park fire most aggressively north, toward Kelowna, it also swept the fire south, threatening the historic Chute Lake Resort, putting Naramata residents on evacuation alert and blanketing Penticton with smoke for the 21st annual Ironman Canada race.

*"There was a real rumble, and it just flashed all
around us and everything went orange, and
then everything was on fire. I was terrified. Everyone
was really scared. There was nowhere to go."*

SHAWN O'REILLY, Kelowna firefighter

FACING PAGE AND BELOW LEFT: Firefighters work amid the flames and smoke near houses destroyed south of Kelowna. *Steve Bosch/ the Vancouver Sun*

ABOVE: Firefighter in action in the Crawford Estates area of Kelowna. *Nick Procaylo/the Province*

At first, Gary Reed refused to abandon his beloved Chute Lake Resort, a bare-bones lodge nestled in the woods and well-used by cyclists on the Kettle Valley Trail. For two days after the area was evacuated, Reed and a dedicated employee hosed down the main building and eight small cabins, but as flames crept ever closer, the two men fled with a firefighting crew August 20. Reed feared the worst but was amazed when he returned the next day to find firefighters—aided by helicopters and heavy equipment—fending off flames. "I was super surprised," said Reed. "They're doing a fantastic job."

Just south of Reed's resort is the picturesque town of Naramata, where the insatiable Okanagan Mountain Park Fire nipped at the town's northern border. "It's really frightening," said Naramata resident Randy Clements. "When the wind came up and pushed the fire in Kelowna's direction, it could just as easily have been us. We're six to eight kilometres from that fire and I'm getting thumb-sized chunks of charcoal. Just imagine how far the live embers are flying."

Residents of 50 of Naramata's 800 homes were ordered to leave August 20; another 500 were temporarily evacuated two days later. "You see the ashes falling. You see the smoke in the sky and you're not sleeping well at night. I've seen how quickly the conifers can go up. It can move very quickly, depending on the wind," said Naramata resident Tony Ramsey, as he prepared to flee with his wife and three children. Added Joann Pfeifer, who runs a day care in her Naramata home: "Even the kids are stressed. They don't understand the devastation, but they're all worried about losing their things."

At Lang Vineyards, on the outskirts of town, all combustible material had been moved away from the winery buildings. "We have 850-litre containers that we're filling with water and putting around the house," said vintner Ross Mirko, adding that the Lang family planned to fight the flames if they threatened the vineyards.

FACING PAGE: At the Cedar Creek winery, bulldozer operator Doug Oliver plows a fire line on the northeast side of Cedar Creek's upper vineyard. *Brian Sprout/ the Vancouver Sun*

BELOW: A bridge along the Kettle Valley Railway was one of many being threatened by the forest fire. The railway is part of the Trans Canada Trail and a popular tourist attraction. *Richard Lam/Canadian Press*

Smoke drifting south from the Okanagan Mountain fire and north from another major blaze near Vaseux Lake also cast a heavy pall over Penticton August 24, forcing organizers to make changes to the routes used for the popular Ironman race. (Tom Evans, 35, placed second in the gruelling competition, even though his family's Naramata house had been put on evacuation alert four days earlier.) The Vaseux fire, which started in an osprey nest on top of a power pole August 22, grew to 3,300 hectares, forcing crews to make control lines with hand tools in the steep Dutton Creek canyon. Roads were soon closed near Okanagan Falls and residents banned from wandering in rural areas near the fire, and the blaze was 100 per cent contained by September 8.

FACING PAGE: Some houses were destroyed while others were untouched by the Okanagan Mountain Park forest fire. *Ian Smith/the Vancouver Sun*

ABOVE: Fire damage in the Crawford Estates area of Kelowna on August 23. *Nick Procaylo/the Province*

THE FIRESTORM was endless in the southern Interior in the summer of 2003. Another major blaze broke out July 16 on Anarchist Mountain, just east of Osoyoos, damaging three buildings and threatening 32 homes, all of which were placed on evacuation alert. In Osoyoos, the Senior Centre assisted residents of the town of 5,000 who fled their homes because they feared the flames were too close. The Anarchist Mountain blaze, ignited by sparks from a vehicle on Highway 3, grew to 1,245 hectares. It would take 10 helicopters and more than 200 firefighters before it was fully contained 11 days later. But it would require far more resources and time to get the massive Okanagan Mountain Park wildfire under control. In the week following the loss of the Kelowna houses, buses were organized to take homeowners back into their neighbourhoods. They peered through its windows at their properties—some still standing, others only ash pits—while clean-up crews tried to make the area inhabitable again. George Scotter's Okaview Road house was still there, but most of his neighbours' homes were gone. "It was very emotional," says Scotter of the bus ride. "We held each other's hands. We leaned on each other's shoulders and we were crying."

Linda and Ken Walker knew as they boarded the bus that the house they built 22 years ago was incinerated. After fleeing the neighbourhood, they had stood on

FACING PAGE: Homes destroyed
by the Okanagan Mountain Park
fire on August 22. *Ian Smith/
the Vancouver Sun*

BELOW: Fire damage in the
Crawford Estates area of Kelowna,
August 23, shows the fickle nature
of the fire. *Nick Procaylo/the Province*

FACING PAGE, TOP: A front porch ornament is all that remains after fire ripped through south Kelowna. *Ian Smith/the Vancouver Sun*

FACING PAGE, BOTTOM: Only a stone archway remains of a home in the Okaview and Curlew area, hit by forest fires August 22. *Ian Smith/ the Vancouver Sun*

BELOW: A burned-out car in Kelowna, ravaged by fire August 22. *Ian Smith/the Vancouver Sun*

"It probably won't sink in until

we see the ashes."

GRAHAM GIBSON, whose Okaview Road

home in Kelowna was destroyed

FACING PAGE: A foundation and charred steps are all that is left of a home destroyed in the Okanagan Mountain Park fire. *Steve Bosch/ the Vancouver Sun*

BELOW: Kelowna building inspectors evaluate the damage. *Ian Smith/the Vancouver Sun*

ABOVE: Kelowna firefighter Shawn O'Reilly describes the challenges he and other firefighters faced while battling forest fires in the Okaview area in Kelowna, August 25. *Richard Lam/Canadian Press*

FACING PAGE: An aluminum gas meter, misshapen from the heat, was produced when this home burned down. *Ian Smith/ the Vancouver Sun*

the western shores of Okanagan Lake—along with hundreds of other mesmerized residents— watching the ridge where their home had stood turn bright red against a dark sky. Linda Walker saved her recipe book and some Christmas decorations, but as she stared at the burned-out property, she thought of other possessions lost to the flames: her favourite furniture, a bedspread her grandmother had embroidered for a wedding present, the cross-stitch her daughter gave her. Ken Walker misses his 1964 stereo and collection of expensive, single-malt Scotch. "Everyone on the bus had a positive attitude, surprisingly. There was no woe-is-me," recalls Linda Walker. In fact, she says, the disaster has brought the neighbours closer.

By Saturday, August 30, eight days after the loss of the houses, all but 70 of the 30,000 evacuees were given the green light to return home. Workers had removed fallen trees, charred electrical wires and damaged telephone poles. Utility companies had restored most of the electricity and gas services, though some residents temporarily returned to dark, cold houses. Others were told to boil their water while health officials continued to test for possible contamination. Regardless, most were happy to begin emptying fridges of rotting food, taking out left-behind trash and protecting properties from looters. After living in a hotel room for a week, Ferguson Sleep was even excited about doing chores at his still-standing home. "I just want to go cut the grass and water the rose bushes," said Sleep, 62, with a wide grin. "It's going to be a pleasure. I'll never complain again for as long as I live about anything. I've got my home."

Jodi Brash thought her home, still intact in the Crawford subdivision, would be covered in dirt and soot, but there was nothing wrong with the house aside from the mild smell of smoke and a dry front-yard pond. "It's almost like we went away on holidays and nothing happened," she recalls.

It was hard to understand the whim of the fickle flames. While some homes were nothing more than mounds of ash, others stood unaffected, complete with

hanging baskets and manicured lawns. "It's just like a bomb went off, but it's so weird because there will be a house in the midst of it that's just completely standing there, nothing wrong with it," said Anne Sullivan, who held her husband's hand as she looked at her levelled Crawford Estate-area home. "It was just surreal."

Some residents were not thrilled to return home, even though their houses had been spared. "It's not a safe place for me yet," said a frightened Inga Clark as she watched helicopters dump water on the blaze near her house. "I wish I could feel at home, but I can't, because there's so much going on in that forest. One of the firefighters still calls it a sleeping monster."

ABOVE: The vinyl has melted on this pool at a property destroyed in the Okanagan Mountain Park fire. *Ian Smith/the Vancouver Sun*

FACING PAGE: Waterfront homes were incinerated by the Okanagan Mountain Park fire, August 22. *Ian Smith/the Vancouver Sun*

Indeed, officials warned that the danger was not past. The wildfire was only 70 per cent contained, and a simple shift in the wind would mean the city was again threatened. "We're trying on one hand to get life back to normal for as many people as possible, but the threat is very much still on the horizon and is very much wind-dependent," said Ron Mattiussi, director of the Kelowna emergency operations centre. "The fire really is still looming on the horizon."

He was right. While no more homes would be lost in Kelowna, the devastation was far from over. The out-of-control Okanagan Mountain Park fire roared into the deep wind funnel of Myra Canyon, devouring 12 of the 18 historic trestle bridges built as part of the Kettle Valley Railway between 1910 and 1916. (Steel decks on two other trestles were damaged.) Considered an engineering marvel, the trestles had been declared a national heritage site in January of 2003. Ed Kruger, who has biked and snowshoed on the trail for 27 years, says the loss of the trestles is akin to losing a family member. "I've talked to some people who have lost their homes, and they were more saddened when the trestles went up," says Kruger. The bridges are mourned for financial, as well as emotional, reasons. The Kettle Valley trail is credited with generating $5 million and drawing 50,000 visitors to the region each year.

BELOW: Firefighter John Kelly lost his house to fire on the outskirts of Kelowna. The following day he was fighting to protect others' homes on his first shift back from vacation. *Chuck Stoody/ Canadian Press*

FACING PAGE: Celeste Ash, front, and friend Miranda Pepper sift through the debris that was once the home Ash lived in with her parents in the Crawford Estates area, Kelowna. *Richard Lam/Canadian Press*

"The icing on the cake, the jewel on the outdoor recreational crown, has always been Myra Canyon," says Craig Henderson of Kettle Valley Trail Tours in Naramata.

Hungry flames gobbled up the trestles' old creosote-coated timbers, some of which were discarded on the valley floor following a restoration project in the early 1990s. They had been sprayed with fire-retardant gel and hosed down with water, but there was little firefighters could do to stop the flames. "It's so smoky and windy in the canyon that it's difficult to work there," said Brian Kempf of the B.C. Forest Service.

In early September, the unpredictable fire forced a second round of evacuations for more than 4,000 residents of the heavily wooded Joe Rich and June Springs communities in south Kelowna. A total of 15,000 more homes were also on evacuation alert after gusty winds shifted the 25,300-hectare fire to within five kilometres of the city. Steve Hidlebaugh, 28, was devastated to leave his new property again. "That's my dream home. That's the house I want to raise my kids in and I'd hate to see it go down in flames. There's nothing you can do, just sit back and watch the show."

Ron Fazio refused to obey the evacuation order after learning his insurance company would not renew his policy because of the fire threat to his property. "We don't have any choice, so we're going to defend the place," he said.

The rest of Kelowna also felt the strain of the continued threat. "We thought this was behind us and the worst was over," said Carol Suhan, of the Kelowna emergency operations centre. Still, the forecast improved a few days later, on September 8, when a light rain fell on the city. It was enough to buoy the spirits of firefighters battling the persistent flames and to permit 4,250 remaining evacuees to return home. The drizzle practically had Kelowna residents dancing in the

ABOVE: After being evacuated for seven days, Ferguson Sleep enjoys watering his roses in the backyard of his McCulloch Road home in Kelowna, saved from the fires. *Brian Sprout/the Vancouver Sun*

FACING PAGE: "I have a house!" exclaims Warren Saari as he emerges from the August 24 meeting where officials informed evacuated residents whether their homes were destroyed or saved. For more than 200 others, the news was not good. *Ian Smith/ the Vancouver Sun*

streets. "We thought we were hallucinating," laughed Karen Cairns. "It's the best news we've had in a long time."

Added Kelowna mayor Walter Gray: "Who would ever think that someone in the Okanagan would want rain? Clouds never looked so good."

Kelowna resident Frank Roughton had been away from his home for two and a half weeks when he returned with the final wave of evacuees. He was grateful to see his 10-year-old Victorian-style house still standing; he was horrified to find it covered in slimy white gunk—a protective fire-retardant gel that forms a thermal layer over a building. "It's ugly, there's white crap everywhere," said Roughton, but "if it saved the house, I'm not going to complain."

Finally, six weeks after the lightning bolt that ignited Squally Point and started the Okanagan Mountain Park blaze, firefighters had the fire fully contained. It had destroyed 25,912 hectares. While some residents met with builders and insurance companies, others made drastic changes to try to protect their rural properties from future wildfires. Yvonne Caldwell paid a tree-cutting service $200 for every pine tree she had decided to remove. "We moved here because of the trees," she mourned. "We told them when we built, 'Leave as many trees as possible.'" But despite living in a construction zone in a vastly altered landscape, most Kelowna and area residents maintained their optimism and sense of humour as they looked forward to life eventually returning to normal.

"We'll all have better views," Okaview resident Jackie Pattison joked darkly, "with all those trees gone."

And in the end, says Lisa Jarrett, who lost her home on Chute Lake Road in Kelowna, the most important outcome of the Kelowna wildfire is that no one was killed. "For every one of us, ultimately the most important thing is life. Right? No one has been hurt. Period. Not a fireman. Not a policeman. It's a miracle," says the mother of two young children, smiling through her tears. "And no house is worth that."

*"I just want to go cut the grass and water the
rose bushes. It's going to be a pleasure.
I'll never complain again for as long as I live about
anything. I've got my home."*

FERGUSON SLEEP, whose Kelowna house was spared

"They're giving it all they've got, [but] the

fire is bigger than the firefighters."

STACEY BASQUE, one of hundreds of rural residents

threatened by the Lamb Creek fire

CRANBROOK & AREA

LAMB CREEK, PLUMBOB MOUNTAIN, NELSON, FERNIE

FACING PAGE: Canadian armed forces firefighter Sgt. Michael Hillman. *Glenn Baglo/the Vancouver Sun*

THE CRANBROOK AREA was both the first and the last of the three B.C. regions ravaged by firestorms in the summer of 2003. By late September, seven major fires and hundreds of smaller ones had chewed through an estimated 35,000 hectares between Nelson and Fernie. Although Kelowna residents expressed relief that no one was killed fighting their massive forest fire, those in the Kamloops area mourned the death of Mission helicopter pilot Ben von Hardenberg, and in Cranbrook there was a community's grief over a double tragedy. On July 16, air-attack pilots Ian Mackay and Eric Ebert died in the line of duty after their aerial bomber went down near the Cranbrook airport. The region's largest infernos, Lamb Creek and Plumbob Mountain, weren't even on the horizon yet. The pilots were responding to one of a number of smaller fires that had broken out near Cranbrook following a thunderstorm.

The morning of July 16 started like most others for Mackay, 41, a father of four from Rossland. He had breakfast at a Kimberley hotel with a "bird-dog" officer—the observer in a smaller plane who would fly ahead and direct his aerial bomber to the fire.

"I talked to the bird-dog officer, and he said Ian was, as usual, calm and in no rush," says Mackay's widow, Laura, a Rossland teacher. "[Ian] said, 'It's a routine drop, it's no big deal, enjoy yourself. Let's just go and get to work.' It was all routine;

very calm, very professional. And then the accident happened." Mackay's four-engine Lockheed Electra bomber crashed just after the plane dumped a load of flame-retardant material on a small fire about 10 kilometres southeast of Cranbrook. RCMP say witnesses saw the tanker make a loop and fly over a set of power lines before it smashed into a mountainside about 1:20 PM.

Mackay and Ebert, 36, of Toronto, were both employees of Edmonton-based Air Spray Ltd.—hired by the provincial government to fight the wildfires in B.C. Despite a company investigation, the cause of the crash may never be known, as the tanker—carrying as much as 8,000 kilograms of fuel—exploded on impact. "The only people who really know what happened are Ian and Eric," says Laura Mackay, whose husband worked in the firefighting business for some 17 years, as a pilot, fire-spotter and smoke-jumper, the daredevils who parachute into forest fires. It was his first season working with Ebert, described by his parents as a man who loved adventure, and the two men got along well.

Ian Mackay, whose father also flew retardant bombers, told his wife he anticipated being busy in the summer of 2003, given that the conditions were ripe for wildfires. But it was a challenge he was up for; he loved his career. "The interface fires he found challenging, and the most rewarding, the houses and sawmills they saved," says Laura. "It's what he loved to do. It was exciting." It was that enthusiasm, and her husband's confidence and natural skills as a pilot, that kept her from worrying every time he left for work or when he flew low over their house at dusk "to say goodnight to the kids," a nine-year-old girl and three sons aged 11 to 16. It's not surprising, perhaps, that since his death Laura has received more than 1,000 letters from people who met him at some point in one of the many areas of his life, perhaps during his aviation career or while sharing his hobbies of heli-skiing and kayaking. "He was an amazing man," says Laura.

Mackay's co-pilot, Eric Ebert, had also worked as a firefighter since he joined Air Spray in 1997 and, again, was someone friends and family described as "amazing."

"He loved B.C.; that job was his life," says Eric's father, Gerry, of the second son he lost to the B.C. outdoors. His elder son, Brian (Bert), a mountain guide, was killed north of Whistler in 1995 after a cornice collapsed beneath him. "Both

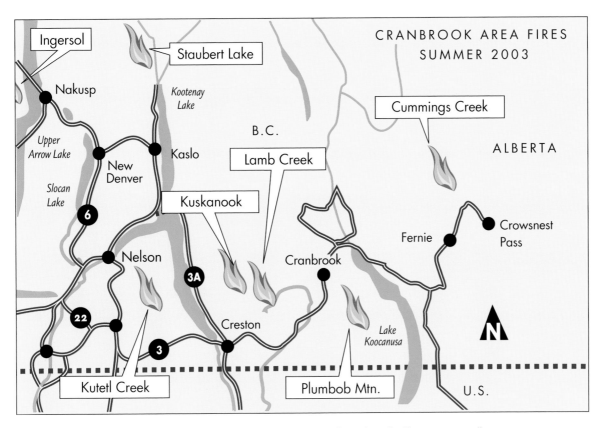

Ingersol

Staubert Lake

Nakusp

Kootenay
Lake

B.C.

Cummings Creek

ALBERTA

Upper
Arrow Lake

Kaslo

New
Denver

Lamb Creek

Slocan
Lake

Kuskanook

6

Crowsnest
Pass

Fernie

Nelson

3A

Cranbrook

22

Creston

3

Lake
Koocanusa

N

Kutetl Creek

Plumbob Mtn.

U.S.

of them knew they were doing dangerous things and what the challenges were," says their father, "but neither one of them would ever have been happy doing a desk job. And I understand. It's something you accept." Still, after Bert's death, Gerry says Eric spoke little about the dangers inherent in low-flying firefighting. "We would get more information about it from his friends."

Shortly after the crash, Gerry Ebert discovered something else he hadn't known about his son: Eric was writing a play. "The first we found out about it was when we were told part of the play was the only thing that survived the crash; pages 25 to 28 arrived in the mail. Somehow or other, the updraft from the fire must have blown them up into the air. Just a few of the pages were recovered, though to tell you the truth; I haven't read them; I haven't got around to doing it." But he says he understands the debt British Columbians feel toward his son and the other pilots who died. "I have a feeling of pride in him."

IAN MACKAY'S PREDICTION of a fiery summer would soon come true. While the fires around Kamloops and, later, Kelowna attracted much of the public and media attention through most of the summer, by the middle of August it was clear the Kootenays—and particularly Cranbrook—were also in peril. One of the major culprits was the Lamb Creek fire, discovered August 7, which would soon dominate

FACING PAGE: Longtime Cranbrook resident Susan Campbell in the process of evacuating her home at Jim Smith Lake, with the help of friends Matthew Clarkson and Ian Bodman. *Brian Clarkson/ the Vancouver Sun*

BELOW: Cranbrook mayor Ross Priest next to a yellow ribbon—the ribbons popped up everywhere to support the fire effort. *Bob Keating/the Province*

the headlines. In addition, a thunderstorm struck the same day with 300 strikes, 50 of which led to the eruption of new fires. Fire officials responded by splitting the region's firefighters into 50 three-man initial-attack crews. Six 20-person crews were reserved to deal with the larger fires. Hundreds of private contractors were also thrown into the mix.

Wildfires were burning near Invermere and in Kootenay National Park north of Radium. Within days, fires had also begun at Ingersol and at Kutetl Creek about 10 kilometres east of Nelson. The ground throughout the region was tinder dry, and the twin hazards of strong winds and lightning strikes were proving as dangerous here as in the Okanagan. Richard Dominy of the B.C. Forest Service admitted there was little that could be done. "The aggressiveness of the fire activity in the last few days has been unprecedented," was how he summed up the situation for reporters. "Fires that we could hold at 100 hectares are now growing to 1,000 and we're still not stopping them."

Cranbrook residents were now beginning to feel the heat from the Lamb Creek fire, as burning embers blew into their yards and fine layers of ash coated their decks. Still, only four families—near Baynes Lake—were evacuated, after being threatened by yet another new fire, on Plumbob Mountain.

On August 14, part of the Lamb Creek fire jumped a fire guard. Its new path didn't threaten any buildings, so fire crews let it go. The first evacuation centre was set up at the Baynes Lake community centre, where it catered to the few families that had been driven out and to holiday campers displaced by the fires in the area. Firefighters caught a well-earned break on August 16 as afternoon showers slowed the progress of the region's major fires. The Plumbob Mountain fire, so threatening in its early stages, was declared 85 per cent contained. But local contractors continued to pound it with helicopters equipped with 500-gallon water buckets. As the fires on both sides of the city sent smoke rolling over Cranbrook, local politicians looked to Kamloops and Kelowna and counted themselves lucky.

ABOVE: Hidden Valley resident George LaBounty watches as an endless cycle of helicopters drop water and fire retardant on a forest fire opposite his home west of Cranbrook. *Ted Jacob/ the Calgary Herald*

By August 20, the 3,000-hectare Lamb Creek fire at Moyie Lake west of Cranbrook had grown to the point that local residents were placed on evacuation alert. The same day, an extreme weather alert forced firefighters to pull back from the borders of some fires. Bob Pfannenschmidt, forest service commander for the area, explained that while guards had been built around the major fires, they were still considered out of control. By August 24, the Kootenays were getting a temporary helping hand from Mother Nature that she denied the Kamloops and Kelowna regions, as a sprinkling of rain fell and temperatures dropped, though more than 700 residents in various parts of the southeast remained under evacuation alert. Next day, the wind picked up again, with spot fires started from flying embers breaking out on the other side of the Lamb Creek guards. On August 26, these outbreaks led to the evacuation of 150 people from some 80 homes in the Munroe Lake area 12 kilometres south of Cranbrook. Twelve helicopters were unable to stem renewed aggression of the Lamb Creek blaze when high temperatures and strong winds drove the flames to within a dozen kilometres of Cranbrook's city limits.

The situation grew more serious by the hour. "Uncontained and out of control," was Pfannenschmidt's succinct assessment. Winds of up to 80 kilometres an hour created spot fires up to 2.5 kilometres ahead of the Lamb Creek blaze. Fire guards were constructed and then abandoned before the racing flames. "The fire is spotting ahead of itself," said Pfannenschmidt. "I can't put people in there at the head of the flanks because the fire will spot over them and then they're trapped between two fires—and that's not where you want to be."

Leanna Spring, 47, was one of those evacuated from Munroe Lake. The fire was burning within 500 metres of her home when she, her husband, Frank, and children, Kylee and Talus, were urged out by RCMP. "We've been doing good so far, but it's like living in a war zone," said Spring, adding that being evacuated was far less stressful than maintaining a daily vigil on the fire's progress.

BELOW: Lumberton resident
Stacey Basque mirrors the feelings
of Cranbrook area citizens with an
homage to firefighters at her home
along Highway 3 east of Cranbrook.
Ted Jacob/the Calgary Herald

"The interface fires he found challenging . . . the most

rewarding, the houses and sawmills

they saved. It's what he loved to do. It was exciting."

LAURA MACKAY, wife of Ian Mackay, killed in an

aerial bomber crash July 16 while fighting a Cranbrook-area fire

By August 28, Cranbrook was truly under siege, with the Lamb Creek fire now covering nearly 10,000 hectares. A thick blanket of smoke settled over the city, while ash rained down onto homes and businesses. Flames could clearly be seen from the city. "It's probably the worst conditions we could hope for," said Cranbrook mayor Ross Priest. "It's not that we're not used to having forest fires around. This one is significantly different."

Throughout the firestorm assault, residents such as Stacey Basque, one of the hundreds of rural residents threatened by the Lamb Creek fire, spoke of their admiration for the firefighters: "They're giving it all they've got, [but] the fire is bigger than the firefighters. I'm thinking some people are going to lose their homes—it's scary," said Basque, whose house in the Lumberton area south of Cranbrook bordered the evacuation zone. The Lamb Creek fire also threatened 36 homes along the eastern shore of Munroe Lake, which were perilously close to the flames. Despite the winds, none were lost, thanks in part to the sprinklers pouring a steady stream of water onto their roofs.

On August 30, local hockey star Scott Niedermayer tried to lift spirits by bringing the Stanley Cup to the Cranbrook RecPlex and to weary fire crews resting at the Bombardier fire camp. "Morale is really, really high today," said Pfannenschmidt following the visit. "It was the talk of the town this morning for sure in camp, and it will be for the rest of their lives." Meanwhile, a brief respite from high winds enabled some evacuees to return briefly to their homes to clean out their fridges. Local police, angered by increasing numbers of "fire tourists," promised to vigorously enforce a 20-kilometre-per-hour no-stopping zone along Highway 3.

As August rolled into September, a series of light winds enabled fire crews to increase their stranglehold on the now largely passive Plumbob and Lamb Creek blazes. More than 500 firefighters and 17 helicopters worked at the fires' perimeters, burning any fuel they might use to surge forward. Crews also aggressively tackled a fire at Kuskanook Creek, some 20 kilometres northeast of Creston. The rapidly growing fire had initially threatened homes on Kootenay Lake. A smaller fire at Cummings Creek northwest of Sparwood also drew attention. A vigorous attack limited the renegade blaze to 1,000 hectares and, by September 8, it was contained.

While the Cranbrook-area fires attracted attention in the southeast, three West Kootenay fires caused severe forest damage and accounted for some racing heartbeats.

The Kutetl fire, 10 kilometres east of Nelson, was the largest, consuming 7,900 hectares. Begun by a lightning strike on August 9, it was eventually contained by mid-September. It burned largely in isolated high country but caused some concern when it approached the communities of Harrop and Proctor in early September. By September 15, it had been contained through the efforts of 250 firefighters and a good dousing of rain.

ABOVE: NHL defenceman Scott Niedermayer holds the Stanley Cup over his head while standing on a fire truck as firefighters surround him at a fire camp in his hometown of Cranbrook, August 30. *Brian Clarkson/Canadian Press*

The Ingersol and Burton fires that broke out in early August on either side of Arrow Lakes, 25 kilometres south of Nakusp, led to evacuation alerts being issued to 450 people, with several actually being forced from their homes. The Ingersol fire burned 6,700 hectares on the west side of Arrow Lake, with Burton Lake consuming 530 hectares. By September 11, both were contained.

The Kuskanook fire on the east shore of Kootenay Lake was a latecomer in the fire season. Beginning on August 27, it led to an evacuation alert for 156 people. At its peak of some 4,832 hectares, it attracted the attention of 250 firefighters. By September 12, the alert was over and all evacuation notices had been rescinded.

By Sunday, September 7, the smoke was clearing and morale throughout the Cranbrook area was improving. It was clear the worst had passed. Monday saw rain, with more showers forecast for the next few days. But one last major fire would be discovered—on September 6 at Staubert Lake, about 40 kilometres southeast of Revelstoke. While there was initial concern for six homes, the fire grew no more than 600 hectares in size and was contained by September 11. Meanwhile, mopping up continued at several fires in the region: Kutetl Creek was contained by September 22, Lamb Creek by September 16, Ingersol by September 11 and Kuskanook by September 16—even Plumbob was mopped up by September 10. Finally, on September 14, 2003, B.C. premier Gordon Campbell lifted the provincewide state of emergency.

"Day by day, week by week, month by month,

Kelowna is bouncing back.

As a community we are already stronger,

and as a city we will be better."

WALTER GRAY, mayor of Kelowna, in early October

EPILOGUE

A S THE FLAMES RETREATED and tender new shoots appeared from beneath the ash-covered ground, the tens of thousands of B.C. residents affected by the summer of 2003's wildfires focused on their own regrowth, on the building of new homes and the making of new plans for the future. Students returned to school, even though some were still on evacuation alert; construction companies and insurance agencies worked long, hard hours to keep up with the onslaught of claims and new business; wineries and orchard owners assessed their soot-covered crops; charities and charitable citizens pulled together to help those left homeless or jobless, and big names in Canada's music business threw benefit concerts that not only raised cash for the needy but raised the collective spirit of the wildfire victims.

"I feel the love, let me tell ya," East Coast music sensation Natalie MacMaster called out to a crowd of 20,000 fans at Kamloops' September 28 Fire on the Mountain aid concert. Organized by Canadian music producer Randall Prescott, and including performers Matthew Good, the Moffatts, Chantal Kreviazuk, Michelle Wright and Prairie Oyster, FIREstock raised some $85,000 for the cause. Vancouver rocker Bryan Adams, along with opening act Colin James, performed a series of concerts in November, while pop diva Cher donated proceeds from her August concert in Vancouver.

FACING PAGE: New life springs from the rubble of a destroyed Kelowna home. *Bill Keay/the Vancover Sun*

113

The aid money was desperately needed. The Insurance Bureau of Canada predicted the summer fires of 2003 could be the second most expensive natural disaster in Canadian history—after 1998's $1.3-billion ice storm in Quebec and eastern Ontario. By fall, the bureau had shelled out more than $200 million in claims to fire victims and expected the figure to be still climbing at year's end. Preliminary estimates put the provincial government's own price tag for the 2003 fire season at $550 million, 10 times more than it had budgeted for, including $400 million for direct firefighting costs, $100 million for emergency services for evacuees and $50 million for clean-up and forest remediation. The figures, warned Victoria, were conservative.

In late October, the federal government committed $100 million in aid money to help B.C. foot the bill for its emergency response and recovery expenditures and reconstruction efforts. Premier Gordon Campbell suggested some of the money could be used for individual cases of hardship. While some complained the provincial and federal governments were tardy in committing aid funds, all applauded volunteer efforts, including the charitable organizations that pitched in immediately. By the fall, the Salvation Army alone had raised $1.1 million in cash—used, in part, to provide each of the 334 families who lost their homes with an emergency cheque of $1,000 and a pre-Christmas buffer of $500. The organization also collected more than $1.2 million in donated goods, enough to cram full three warehouses in the Interior. Its relief efforts were so successful, in fact, that the charity eventually appealed to British Columbians to stop donating goods; it had more than could be used. As well, the Red Cross raised $3.1 million to assist 200 families in Louis Creek and Barriere and 111 more in Kelowna with basic needs. "In certain circumstances, we pay the rent and make damage deposits if they have no insurance or other means of assistance," said Kelowna Red Cross manager Phil Bond.

In early August, 16 transport trucks organized by CanWest Global, Telus and London Drugs delivered emergency supplies such as sleeping bags, pillows, water,

FACING PAGE: Hillary Brydon shows her excitement over plans for a new home with her parents, Ron and Lynn Brydon. *Bill Keay/ the Vancouver Sun*

BELOW: Ground Zero for the Brydon family—left to right are Ron, Lynn, eight-year-old Hillary and 14-year-old Courtney. The family's southeast Kelowna home was destroyed after a forest fire tore through their neighbourhood. *Bill Keay/the Vancouver Sun*

BELOW: A doll's hand lies amongst the ruins of the Brydons' burned-out Kelowna home. *Bill Keay/ the Vancouver Sun*

FACING PAGE: Doll's face found among the rubble of the Brydon family home in Kelowna. *Bill Keay/ the Vancouver Sun*

FACING PAGE, TOP: The remains of a bicycle and lawnmower, Kelowna. *Bill Keay/the Vancouver Sun*

FACING PAGE, BOTTOM: A burned, misshapen golf club stands as testimony to the Kelowna fire's force. *Bill Keay/the Vancouver Sun*

BELOW: Burned hammer and nails left in the ashes of a Kelowna home. *Bill Keay/the Vancouver Sun*

NORTH COWICHAN

FIRE DEPARTMENT
CROFTON

PESTIGIA NULLA RETRORSUM

INCORPORATED 1873

light clothing, hygiene products and 4,000 long-distance calling cards to families forced to flee their homes. "The response from the people and businesses in British Columbia was incredible," says Dennis Skulsky, CanWest's B.C. Mainland general manager and publisher of the *Vancouver Sun* and *Province* newspapers. In Kelowna, firefighters and the RCMP sold baseball caps and T-shirts to raise money. The public gave nearly $100,000 to help the SPCA look after 3,000 animals left homeless. Even more donations rolled in from diverse groups, including large corporations, B.C.'s Chinese community, a Kelowna radio station selling yellow ribbons and two children who raised $12.59 with a lemonade stand. Still others travelled to the Interior to try to boost the spirits of fire victims, including six high-profile members of the Vancouver Canucks who flew to Kelowna. "After watching it on the news and reading about it in the papers, you knew how bad it was, but actually seeing it first-hand blows you away," said centre Brendan Morrison.

By far the most successful independent fund-raising drive was the North Thompson Relief Fund, established by George Evans. The Kamloops auto dealer began with a modest goal of raising $200,000. Three months later he had collected $2.53 million to assist 114 families in Louis Creek, McLure and Barriere, a predominantly blue-collar area where 72 homes were lost and many were left jobless. An estimated 30 to 50 per cent of North Thompson residents did not have insurance; most had no extra cash to get back on their feet. Evans purchased supplies for eight new houses in Louis Creek, which were built by volunteers from church groups for those without insurance; the fund also bought the North Star Mobile House Park and 12 new mobile homes to provide residences for other uninsured people.

Nine businesses were incinerated in the North Thompson, including the Tolko sawmill, which largely sustained Louis Creek and Barriere with employment for some 180 staff and 150 contractors. The community was hit hard when Tolko announced it would not rebuild, and by the fall only a handful of those workers had found new jobs. "Our funds are going to be used not only to rebuild homes but also to stabilize the economy," said Evans.

FACING PAGE: Crofton firefighter Jason Rowley joins the fight against the Okanagan Mountain Park fire. *Gerry Kahrmann/the Province*

ABOVE: A field of thanks for the men and women fighting the summer fires. *Ian Smith/the Vancouver Sun*

ABOVE: Firefighters Jean Yves Jacob, left, and Ron Peterson of Armstrong work on hot spots near a house in suburban Kelowna August 25. *Chuck Stoody/ Canadian Press*

Jill Hayward and her husband, Bob, had insurance to replace their home but needed help to rebuild their cattle ranch in Louis Creek. "[The fire] was like living in your own disaster movie," said a grateful Hayward. "It's just unimaginable to think that all of these people are trying to help our people."

STILL, THREE MONTHS after fire devastated the North Thompson small towns of Louis Creek and Barriere, construction had begun on only 20 new homes to replace the 72 lost in the fires. Real estate agent Kathy Campbell, a fire victim, was furious that owners of high-end homes in Kelowna seemed to be getting more cooperation from insurance companies and government. "Kelowna is booming, and we're bust," she said.

In Kelowna, 238 houses were lost, but most homeowners were professionals with insurance and rainy-day funds in the bank. Two months after the Okanagan Mountain Park fire, permits had been issued for 191 charred ruins to be demolished, while 30 applications were processed for new homes to be built. The homes lost were worth on average $350,000, but outbuildings, furnishings, other personal belongings and living expenses were expected to inflate each insurance claim to between $600,000 and $700,000. "We're going to have a mini-boom," said Jim Morris, president of the Kelowna branch of the Canadian Home Builders Association. "It's a tremendous amount of funds coming in."

As those with insurance made plans to rebuild, some struggled with renewing their policies; others struggled to comprehend them. Ron Brydon laboured to remember every item in his now-vanished Kelowna house while visiting endless stores to research replacement costs. "It takes hours and hours and hours. This is a royal pain in the ass," he said. "I thought the process would be simpler." The contractor Brydon hired hoped to finish building his house in six months. But the sudden need for hundreds of new homes in the region led to a dearth of skilled workers required for everything from toxic soot removal to construction. The shortage was

BELOW: B.C. Forest Service firefighter Todd Nessman works at night. *Ian Smith/the Vancouver Sun*

"It was like the end of the world. We don't

know how we can ever thank all the firefighters.

We are indebted forever."

KRYS ROCHFORT, whose Crawford-area home

in Kelowna was saved

FACING PAGE: Firefighters travelled from all over B.C. to help fight the Okanagan Mountain Park blaze. Left to right: Greg Schalk, Bob Seigmann and Kevin Thompson from the North Vancouver Fire Department. *Gerry Kahrmann/ the Province*

BELOW: Heartfelt "Thank you firefighters" sign erected by Tony D'Andrea and friends on Dilworth Mountain in Kelowna, August 24. *Nick Procaylo/the Province*

expected to increase the costs of construction and delay completion dates, in some cases, for many months. In all, 334 houses and 10 businesses were destroyed: in Kelowna, the numbers totalled 238 houses and one business; in Louis Creek, Barriere and McLure, 72 houses and nine businesses; in McGillivray (including Chase and Sun Peaks), 20 homes; in Osoyoos, three homes and in Falkland, one home.

Former Manitoba premier Gary Filmon, hired by Premier Campbell, promised to conduct a $500,000 "no-holds-barred review" of the summer of fires, to analyze fire-prevention strategies, emergency response, public communication plans, the role of volunteers and the frameworks used for federal assistance. One of the issues Filmon was expected to review was the allegation that B.C. was tardy in following the recommendations of a dire 2001 auditor general's report. It had warned that years of undergrowth should be removed from the province's forest floors to reduce the risk of catastrophic wildfires. Only after the 2003 fires, critics charged, had the government announced it would start a controlled-burn program to eliminate some of the fuel in the bush. A lawyer was hired by one now-homeless Kelowna family to investigate the possibility of suing the B.C. government for negligence.

B.C.'s premier flew to Louis Creek and Barriere in early August, but most politicians waited to visit the region until after the Okanagan Mountain Park fire had wreaked its havoc. Those who delayed included Prime Minister Jean Chrétien, his expected successor, Paul Martin, federal defence minister John McCallum and Governor General Adrienne Clarkson—raising another complaint by Kamloops-area residents that their loss was overshadowed by Kelowna's. In mid-October, Clarkson awarded six firefighters medals for 20 years of "exemplary service." But before her visit, the weary president of the Barriere food bank—which was feeding 300 people in July and an estimated 1,600 by fall—quipped that her community didn't need more politicians shaking hands but more hand-outs. "Ask the governor general to bring a case of macaroni and cheese with her," said Brenda Lavis.

FACING PAGE, TOP LEFT:
Vancouver singer Matthew Good
at the Fire on the Mountain benefit
press conference. *Don MacKinnon/
Sterling News*

FACING PAGE, TOP RIGHT: Singer
Michelle Wright entertains thousands at the Fire on the Mountain
concert at Sport Mart Place,
in Kamloops September 27.
Don MacKinnon/Sterling News

FACING PAGE, BOTTOM: Patricia
Conroy and Tracey Brown were
among the stars playing at the
Fire on the Mountain concert.
Don MacKinnon/Sterling News

HARD-HIT FIRE VICTIMS were also miffed that the provincial government could not reach an agreement with Tolko to rebuild the mill in Louis Creek. Tolko's not re-building would have lasting effects on the viability of Louis Creek and Barriere, said Bill Kershaw, Barriere's representative on the Thompson-Nicola Regional District council. "I believe we can survive it because we have a lot of stability to the community. But it's going to be hard on every business in town." As elsewhere in the province, the economic impact of the fires would be felt long after the last flame was extinguished.

Another blow was the damage done to the historic Kettle Valley Railway. The Okanagan Mountain Park fire destroyed 12 of the rail line's wooden trestles and damaged steel decks on two others; only four of the 18 bridges remain undamaged. Culturally and recreationally significant, the trestles had pumped $5 million into the local economy by drawing 50,000 visitors to the region each summer. "Little towns like Beaverdell, Rock Creek and Midway along the KVR are certainly going to feel a big hit," said Craig Henderson of Kettle Valley Trail Tours and Shuttles in Naramata. The company lost some 25 per cent of its revenue after the fires and was forced to lay off two employees. A committee was formed to study rebuilding the trestles, aided by a technical assessment by CP Rail. Reconstruction was estimated at $30 million; it's unclear how long rebuilding would take.

Other Interior tourism operators, including Sun Peaks Resort near Kamloops, were equally stymied by cancellations during the high-fire season. A combination of bone-dry conditions and numerous wildfires also forced forestry companies to shut down operations across B.C.'s southern Interior in the late summer, prompting layoffs of at least 3,000 harvest workers and some 1,000 millwrights, a drop in production of about 20 per cent, and rising timber prices. Meanwhile, plans were made to salvage the hundreds of thousands of trees left standing in forests decimated by B.C.'s worst-ever wildfire season, with reforestation scheduled for the spring of 2004.

Throughout the region, fruit farmers struggled to harvest crops damaged by the smoke, fire or ash, or those neglected because workers were under evacuation notice at the critical time for picking. St. Hubertus lost its wine shop, cellar and

ABOVE: Jamie Collins, left, and Jamie Brulotte of Service Master set footings for the foundation of a home for Joan and Tom Thompson at Louis Creek. Watching the process is Joan and her son Mark (at top right of the photo). Joan and her husband, Tom, were married in the backyard of their Louis Creek home less than two weeks before fire ripped through the area. *Murray Mitchell/the Province*

office along with its entire crop when flames blew through the Kelowna winery. Other vineyards were threatened but not damaged and, ironically, reported a bumper harvest of grapes following the hot, dry summer. St. Hubertus owner Andy Gebert vowed to rebuild and has been grateful for the support offered by his competitors. In return, Gebert is raising money for a fire-relief fund by hastily marketing two new wines: Glowing Amber Chardonnay and Fireman's Red.

Stories like Gebert's are scattered across the Interior: a natural disaster devastating the land, but bringing out the best in most of the people caught up in it. Thousands, for example, volunteered to give shelter to evacuees, even though they were often total strangers. People like Wendy Munson, who in late August had nine vehicles, two horses, eight dogs, seven evacuees and the five members of her own family at her Kelowna home. "We all have rotating showers, so it works out," she said.

Other communities rallied around weddings that were interrupted by Mother Nature. Pat Smith had to flee his Barriere home August 1, just days before his daughter Janine's backyard wedding. The family grabbed Smith's suit, his wife's dress and his daughter's wedding ensemble but left behind the 10-kilogram turkey and $2,000 in wedding food. Two days later, Janine was married with a hastily arranged reception at a Kamloops hotel. "It was better that we went ahead with it," says Smith. "We gave people something to celebrate, and everyone had a good time."

Another evacuated couple, D.J. Bryan and his wife, Pierrette, took their vows at the groom's grandparents' farm in Vavenby near Clearwater, even though a wildfire cut the electricity, kept half of the 120 guests from attending and forced the caterer to cancel. Not one to be defeated, Bryan's grandmother dug up potatoes from her garden for a salad and barbecued the salmon from her freezer for a candlelight dinner. Guests gave up their motel rooms to evacuees and made do with campers, vans and tents. "It was absolutely a beautiful wedding," says Bryan's father, Barry Kuypers.

BELOW: Burned forest surrounds homes being rebuilt at Louis Creek. Kendall Cave, of Barriere-based Ken's Construction, works on a roof on one of the first rebuild projects at Louis Creek. *Murray Mitchell/the Province*

School districts were also under the gun to provide a stable start to the school year despite so much uncertainty in their communities. The week before school began in Kelowna, three schools were in the evacuation zone, and 3,500 students and 700 staff had been evacuated from their homes. High schools in Barriere and Chase had students return late for classes because they were among the volunteers fighting the fires. There were also 400 army personnel sleeping in tents on the school grounds of Chase Secondary.

There were countless stories of strangers helping strangers in a time of need. Thirty volunteers helped Connie Miller pack up her business, Terra Botanica Products Ltd., and ferry it across Arrow Lake when her West Kootenay home was threatened by a fire in September. Miller set up shop temporarily in a closed elementary school in Nakusp. "It's not something I would like to experience again any time soon, but I guess something good came out of it. Everybody pulled together in a crisis," she says. Still, as well-intentioned as people were, families were cramped in hotel rooms, evacuees were antsy to be in their own homes again, and volunteers were burning out. "We've been running on adrenaline and coffee," Kelowna mayor Walter Gray said in late August. "But the energy is beginning to wane, and we're still going to need those volunteers and professionals to rebuild people's lives and homes."

Not everyone, of course, rushed to help out. Police investigated several reports of looters and gawkers. Dennis Zinger returned to his Pritchard home to find it ransacked by thieves who took jewellery, a chainsaw and a vehicle. "It's bad enough to be evacuated, [and] then to come home and be treated this way by the scum of the earth," fumed Zinger.

RCMP in Kelowna constantly warned boaters to stay out of the way of aerial tankers and helicopters scooping water from Okanagan Lake. Residents of burned-out neighbourhoods in that city complained of "fire tourists" driving down their

ABOVE: Prime Minister Jean Chrétien shakes hands with Kelowna mayor Walter Gray as they walk to a press conference in Kelowna, August 24. Kelowna fire chief Gerry Zimmerman and B.C. premier Gordon Campbell accompany them. *Chuck Stoody/Canadian Press*

FACING PAGE, TOP: Kelowna fire chief Gerry Zimmermann, poking fun at the visiting Paul Martin, holds up a homemade bumper sticker that reads: "Gerry Zimmerman for Prime Minister." *David Wylie/Sterling News*

FACING PAGE, BOTTOM: Prime Minister Jean Chrétien and B.C. premier Gordon Campbell thank the Armed Forces. *Chuck Stoody/Canadian Press*

ABOVE: The rebuilding of burned-out homes in Louis Creek, near Barriere. *Murray Mitchell/the Province*

FACING PAGE: Reminders of the devastating fire remain as the reconstruction process begins at Louis Creek. *Murray Mitchell/ the Province*

streets to gawk at the despair. "I don't think the people around here are emotionally ready for tour buses," said Ken Fisher, whose home survived on a street where many did not. But the fire victims, for the most part, vowed to remain in their communities despite burned trees in their backyards and nagging concerns that the fires would start again. "We got scared the first week we started thinking about re-building," says Michael Fraser, who lost his Kelowna house. "We said, 'Do we really want our master bedroom overlooking these burnt matchsticks that are sitting there?' [But] I cannot stress how much our community is a community." Added Celeste Ash, also of Kelowna, "It's sad, but at the same time it's exciting, because this whole neighbourhood is going to be new and we're going to have lots of house-warming parties. We've really all come together."

AFTER THE HOUSES are rebuilt, the trestles replaced and trees replanted, perhaps the most lasting memory of the summer of 2003 will be the firefighters who became heroes in the eyes of many citizens. An estimated 10,000 people—firefighters from across Canada, members of the B.C. Forest Service, military soldiers and re-servists and other emergency staff—battled the blazes. Equipment such as giant Alberta-made fire trucks used in the Gulf War and three fire-bombing aircraft from New Brunswick were donated. "It was like the end of the world," says Kelowna resident Krys Rochfort of the fires. "We don't know how we can ever thank all the firefighters. We are indebted forever."

Calgary firefighter Paul Graf and two of his colleagues drove to Kelowna without being asked. "[We] just came out when we heard firefighters were losing homes and, we said, 'Whatever it takes to help, we'll do it.'" Kathryn Sikkes, a 20-year-old university student who for three summers fought fires as a seasonal worker with the B.C. Forest Service, emerged from the burning bush near Kelowna each day covered in soot but proud of her demanding work. "I love it; I wouldn't want to be anywhere else," she says. "Your job is always exciting. You get to travel. You get to work in the outdoors."

But the long, smoky days took their toll. In Cranbrook, a mysterious illness hit 107 firefighters, which doctors believed may have been a virus attacking their

"I think we looked at that sheet three times

before we could believe it."

LINDSAY MCDONALD, after learning that fire had destroyed

the homes of three members of his family

ABOVE: Paramedics Taylor Sholdice and Debra Pion prepare fresh fruit for the firefighters at the staging point on Chute Lake Road and Lakeshore Drive, Kelowna. *Ian Smith/the Vancouver Sun*

RIGHT: Danny Bryant, of Telus, unloading donations from a truck in Kamloops. *Allan Fedorak/ the Vancouver Sun*

ABOVE: Firefighters create a bucket brigade to unload a pickup truck full of beer—donated to the firefighters by the Brewery Winery Distillery Workers Local 300, Molson and Labatts. *Gerry Kahrmann/the Province*

LEFT: Vancouver Canucks Trevor Linden (pictured), Todd Bertuzzi, Markus Naslund, Dan Cloutier, Brendan Morrison and Johan Hedberg visit Canadian Forces personnel with Operation Peregrine in Kelowna, September 14. *Sgt. David McCord/Canadian Forces*

FACING PAGE: A Kettle Valley
Railway trestle in flames.
Bill Atkinson/pilot

smoke-filled lungs. "These guys are exhausted and tired, exposed to high levels of heat and dust in the air. It's dangerous, hard, heavy work. They've been doing it for a long time," said Dr. Perry Kendall, B.C.'s provincial health officer. Nine Kelowna firefighters also fell ill, many diagnosed with high blood pressure after fighting the firestorms.

As New York mayor Rudolf Giuliani has remained etched in people's minds after the 2001 U.S. terrorists attacks, Kelowna fire chief Gerry Zimmermann became the public face of B.C.'s summer of terror. The folksy chief repeatedly boosted the spirits of his staff and his city, often crying at press conferences while discussing community support—including the two small children pulling a wagon full of potato chips, cookies, flowers and beer on ice to the fire hall—or detailing the battles waged by the firefighters. "We've never been stronger. We're going to keep chasing this thing until it's done," said a weary Zimmermann, who often slept at the local fire hall because he too had been evacuated from his home.

By mid-September, the provincewide state of emergency that had been in effect since August 2 was lifted, the backcountry travel ban rescinded, and only one small group of B.C. residents was under evacuation alert. Yet the battle continued for firefighters deep in the bush, where officials advised it would likely take the first snowfall to snuff out the last flame. Since the first blaze erupted April 1, B.C. had already fought a staggering 2,511 fires and lost 266,135 hectares to the rampaging infernos. By late October, 238 of those fires still smouldered in the forests, stubbornly refusing to die despite torrential rainfalls.

Finally, after a summer of minimal precipitation, the skies opened in October and instigated yet another B.C. disaster—enormous floods on the coast that swamped communities in the Howe Sound and the Fraser Valley, claiming four lives, forcing 800 people from their homes and causing millions of dollars in damage. Yet as they rose out of the ashes, heroes also emerged from the deep waters engulfing the coast. It was as Frank Ambrosio said, as he sifted through the charred remains of his Kelowna home, looking for the wedding ring he forgot to put on his finger before a firestorm devoured his house: "We'll rebuild. We're going to rebound. We're a little bruised, but we'll be back."

*"It's totally disheartening. Human life
is the number one priority, but to have something so
historically important be lost is devastating."*

KIRK HUGHES, B.C. Forest Service

information officer, on the loss of the Kettle Valley trestles

ACKNOWLEDGEMENTS

WRITING

CHARLES ANDERSON A graduate of Cambridge University, Charles Anderson moved to Canada in 1979. He attended the journalism program at Vancouver Community College and began reporting for the *Province* in 1984. An award-winning general assignment reporter, he covers a wide range of subjects with a special emphasis on the environment.

LORI CULBERT Lori Culbert has an English degree from Queen's University and a journalism diploma from Humber College in Toronto. She has been a journalist for 12 years and has worked for seven newspapers across Canada. She joined the *Vancouver Sun* in 1997 and has won several journalism awards.

PHOTO EDITING

NICK PROCAYLO London-born Nick Procaylo began his photography career in the mid-1980s. Based in Vancouver and London during the 1990s, he travelled extensively, covering stories for various magazines and news agencies. He joined the *Province* in 2000.

IAN SMITH Ian Smith grew up with a passion for taking pictures and has been a news photographer for 25 years. The past 18 years of his photojournalism career have been spent with the *Vancouver Sun*.

Anderson, Culbert, Procaylo and Smith covered the 2003 forest fires for the *Vancouver Sun* and *Province* newspapers.

RESEARCH

KATE BIRD In addition to her work as a researcher for the *Vancouver Sun* and *Province* newspapers, Pacific Newspaper Group librarian Kate Bird has worked on a variety of special projects, including the *Vancouver Sun's Frontier Women* series and the *Millennium Series* for the *Province,* which was made into the book *The Way We Were*.

EDITING

SHELLEY FRALIC In her 25 years at the *Vancouver Sun,* Shelley Fralic has reported on, and edited, every topic—from sports and features to religion and politics. She is currently the *Sun's* executive editor and writes a weekly column.

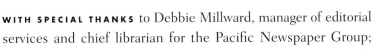

WITH SPECIAL THANKS to Debbie Millward, manager of editorial services and chief librarian for the Pacific Newspaper Group; Wendy Nordvik-Carr, *Vancouver Sun* executive assistant; and Frank Myrskog, *Vancouver Sun* graphic designer.

SOURCES

B.C. Forest Service
Canadian Press
CanWest News Service
The *Cranbrook Daily Townsman*
The *Kamloops Daily News*

The *Province*
The *Vancouver Sun*
Sterling News Service
Wildfire News Web site,
B.C. Ministry of Forests